THE BIG BOOK OF QUESTIONS & ANSWERS

THE BIBLE

AS TOLD IN THE OLD TESTAMENT

Contributing Writers:
David M. Howard, Jr., Ph. D.
Bob Phillips
Carol Richards

Consultant:
Gary M. Burge, Ph. D.

PUBLICATIONS INTERNATIONAL, LTD.

Louis Weber, C.E.O.
Publications International, Ltd.
7373 N. Cicero Avenue
Lincolnwood, Illinois 60646

Permission is never granted for commercial purposes.

Manufactured in the U.S.A.

8 7 6 5 4 3 2 1

ISBN 1-56173-467-5

Library of Congress Catalog Card Number 92-60583

Consultant:
Gary M. Burge is an associate professor in the Department of Biblical and Theological Studies at North Park College. He holds a Ph.D. in New Testament from King's College of The University of Aberdeen in Scotland and a Master of Divinity from Fuller Theological Seminary. He is a member of the Biblical Archaeology Society.

Contributing Writers:
David M. Howard, Jr. is an associate professor of Old Testament and Semitic Languages at Trinity Evangelical Divinity School, and holds a Ph.D. in Near Eastern Studies from the University of Michigan. His writing credits include contributions to *The International Standard Bible Encyclopedia, Anchor Bible Dictionary,* and *Peoples of the Old Testament World* and is a member of the Society of Biblical Literature and the Institute for Biblical Research.

Bob Phillips is the author of over thirty books, ranging in subject matter from Bible trivia to family relationships. He has a Bachelor's Degree in Christian Education from Biola University and a Master's Degree in Counseling from California State at Fresno. He is a licensed marriage, family, and child counselor.

Carol Richards is a diaconal minister of Christian education in the United Methodist Church, and has written student and teacher curriculum for the church's publishing house, the Graded Press. She has been a teacher and is currently program and education coordinator at Corona United Methodist Church.

Illustrated by:
T. F. Marsh
Joe Veno

A: God caused a storm because Jonah was not doing what God told him to do. When Jonah was thrown into the sea the storm calmed down.

CONTENTS

BIBLE STORIES

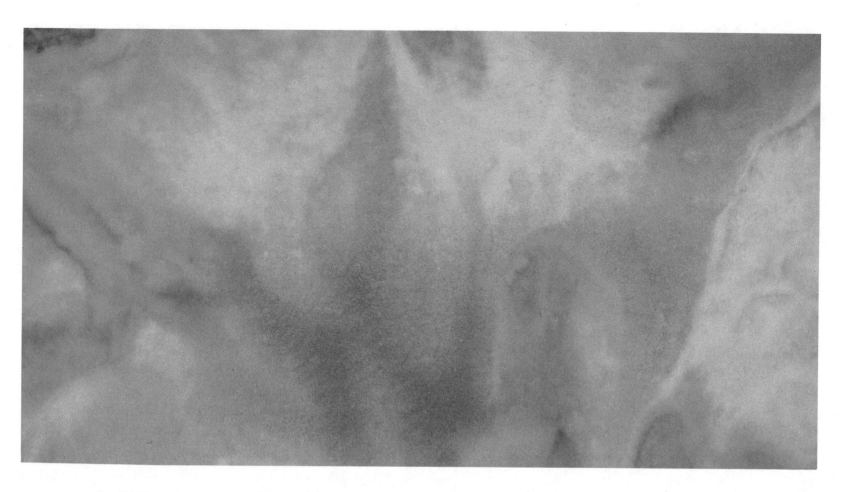

Q: What was it like before our world was created?

A: The Bible tells us that the earth had no shape and that a roaring, raging ocean covered everything. The wind howled and there was total darkness. There were no stars, no moon, no flowers, and no people; just windy, wet darkness. The power of God moved over the emptiness.

Q: What did God create first?

A: The first thing God created was light. Then God separated the light from the darkness and called it day. He called the darkness night. God made light on the first day.

Q: Is there more than one creation story?

A: Yes. Ancient people everywhere had creation stories. Humans have always wondered where they came from and how the world started.

Q: What did God create on the second day?

A: God made a dome to separate the waters on the earth from the waters above. God called the dome the sky. Early people didn't know that the earth was round. They believed it was in layers, like a three-story house. The people believed the dome—or sky—was solid and that it kept back the waters above it.

Q: When were land, plants, and animals created?

A: God was very busy on the third day. Before there could be plants and animals, there had to be dry land. So God gathered up the waters into the seas and made the dry land rise up. This made a place for fruits and vegetables to grow. On the fourth day God ordered the sun and the moon to be put in the sky.

Q: Did God create dinosaurs?

A: On the fifth day God created all kinds of creatures: birds and bugs, worms and weasels, lions and leopards, and, yes, dinosaurs.

Q: Why were people created?

A: God created humans to have a relationship with him. That's what it means to be created in God's image. We don't look like God, but God wants a special loving relationship with us.

Q: What did God do when he was finished?

A: God looked at all his work and was pleased. All creation was very good. So God rested on the seventh day. God blessed this day. That is why we rest every seventh day also.

Q: How did Adam and Eve get their names?

A: *Adam* comes from a Hebrew word that means "human." It was used for both men and women. Adam also means "coming from the earth." *Eve* probably means "living," which may have come to mean "mother."

Q: Why do pictures show Adam and Eve dressed in leaves?

A: Adam and Eve disobeyed God and ate fruit from a forbidden tree. Then they realized they were naked so they picked fig leaves to cover themselves.

Q: What did Adam and Eve tell God about eating the fruit?

A: Adam said that he had eaten some fruit, but he tried to blame Eve. Then Eve blamed the serpent in the garden. Eating the fruit helped Adam and Eve understand good and evil, so they were ashamed.

Q: How did God punish Adam and Eve?

A: God sent them out of the garden. God told the man that he would have to work hard to grow food. The woman would have to work hard bearing children.

Q: Who were Eve's children?

A: Cain was Eve's first son. He grew up to be a farmer. Her next son was named Abel and he kept sheep. Later Seth was born.

Q: Why did Cain get angry?

A: The brothers made a special offering to God. Cain brought some of his crops and Abel brought the very best of his sheep. God liked Abel's offering more than Cain's. Cain was angry, but God told him to do better.

Q: What did Cain do to Abel?

A: Cain decided to get even with his brother Abel. So Cain asked his brother to meet him in the nearby field. Cain then killed Abel. When God asked Cain where Abel was, Cain said,"Am I supposed to watch my brother all the time?" God knew what Cain had done.

Q: What did God do to Cain?

A: God told Cain that his crops would not grow right. Cain would have to wander. Cain cried out that no one liked wanderers. So God put a mark on Cain to let people know that they must not kill him.

Q: Why did Noah build the ark?

A: God was angry with everyone except Noah and his family. God thought everyone else was behaving badly. Noah listened as God explained how to make the ark. Noah knew the ark would need to carry his family and 2 of some kinds of animals and 14 of other animals (for food). God was going to send a great flood.

Q: What did the ark look like?

A: It must have looked very odd, more like a floating house than a boat. Of course, it wasn't meant to sail away on long voyages. It only had to float long enough to keep everyone and everything safe. The ark was longer than a football field and only about half as wide. Noah covered the ark with tar to keep everything dry.

Q: What happened when the flood came?

A: Noah, his family, and the animals were all on the ark before the flood started. It began to rain, then the waters rose. The rain continued for 40 days, until even the mountains were covered. All the living things, except those on the ark, died in the flood.

Q: How did Noah know when it was safe to leave the ark?

A: It took a few months for the water to go down. To find out if it was safe, Noah sent out first a raven, then a dove. The dove flew around and could not find a place to land so it came back. After seven days Noah sent a dove out again. This time it came back with a fresh olive branch. At last! Noah made everyone wait another week before sending out the dove again. This time it did not return—it had found a home.

Q: What did Noah do first after they left the ark?

A: Noah wanted to thank God for keeping his family safe. He built an altar and all of Noah's family worshiped God. God was very pleased with Noah because he had obeyed God.

Q: How did God show he was happy with Noah?

A: God decided that even though humans might be foolish and do wrong things, he would never again destroy all living things by a flood. There would be spring, summer, fall, and winter.

Q: What sign of this promise did God give?

A: The rainbow arching across the sky after a storm is a sign of the covenant or promise God made with Noah and all living things.

Q: What was the Tower of Babel?

A: The Tower of Babel was a ziggurat, which is something like a pyramid with straighter sides and steeper steps. It was made of bricks baked hard and held together with tar.

Q: Who built the tower?

A: Noah's grandchildren and great grandchildren built the tower. At that time all people had one language and they all lived in the same place. These people had moved slowly east to look for a place to settle. When they came to a broad plain they decided to stop and build their homes.

Q: Why did they build the tower?

A: They wanted to be famous. They decided to build a city, then they built the tower.

Q: What did God think about the tower?

A: God came down to see what the people were doing. God looked at the city and at the tower. If these people could build a city and a tower, there would be no stopping them! God thought they might become too proud. So God mixed up their language so people spoke different languages.

Q: Are Sodom and Gomorrah places or people?

A: They were two of the five cities known as "the cities of the plain" in Bible times. We believe they were at the south end of the Dead Sea.

Q: Why were they destroyed?

A: God watched how the people in Sodom and Gomorrah were living and he was unhappy with them. The people were sinful and evil. They got drunk, and they were mean to each other.

Q: What happened to the people who lived there?

A: God would save anyone who loved God and was obedient. But only Lot and his family loved God. No one else believed God would destroy the city by raining sulfur and fire. Everyone except Lot and his family were killed in the fires.

Q: Did Lot and his family escape?

A: Lot and his family were warned to run as fast as they could and not to look back. Lot's wife, however, was sad to leave these bad places. She turned around to see what happened to Sodom. When she looked back she was turned into a pillar of salt.

Q: Why is Abraham so important?

A: God made a covenant, or promise, to Abraham. If Abraham would trust and obey God, God would make Abraham the father of many nations.

Q: How many children did Abraham and Sarah have?

A: Abraham and Sarah had no children. They were both very old. Sarah was 90 years old and Abraham was 100! When God made his covenant with Abraham, he promised that Sarah would have a son. She had a son, Isaac.

Q: Did Abraham keep his part of the covenant?

A: Abraham obeyed God. One day God told Abraham to build an altar and offer Isaac as a sacrifice. Abraham must have felt terrible! But he trusted God. He took Isaac to a mountain and built an altar.

Q: Why would God ask for Isaac as a sacrifice?

A: God was testing Abraham. God wanted to see if Abraham would obey. God never wants parents to hurt their children. At the last moment God's angel told Abraham to stop. There was a ram caught by its horns in a bush. This was the sacrifice God really wanted Abraham to make!

Q: Did Isaac grow up and marry?

A: Abraham and his family were blessed by God and grew rich as Isaac grew up. They had large flocks of sheep and goats. When it was time for Isaac to marry, Abraham did not want Isaac to marry a girl from a nearby family. They were living in Canaan, the land God promised. But their neighbors did not worship God. Abraham had a plan.

Q: What was Abraham's plan?

A: Abraham sent a trusted servant to where their distant relatives lived. Abraham told the servant to find a good wife for Isaac. The servant prayed that God would show him the right person. The servant took bracelets, a nose ring, and other jewelry to give her as gifts.

Q: Did the servant find a wife for Isaac?

A: The servant met Rebekah. She was lovely and thoughtful. She offered to get water for the servant's camels. The servant knew this was a sign from God. He put the jewelry on Rebekah and asked her to take him to her family. The servant and Rebekah's family talked a long time and the marriage was arranged. Rebekah went to Canaan to marry Isaac.

19

Q: Who were Jacob and Esau?

A: Jacob and Esau were the sons of Isaac and Rebekah. Esau was born first and was red and hairy. Jacob was born hanging on to Esau's heel. As they grew, Esau liked to be outside with his father hunting or caring for their flocks. Esau was Isaac's favorite and Jacob was Rebekah's favorite.

Q: What was Jacob like?

A: Jacob was a quiet man who helped his mother, Rebekah. He stayed around the tents where the family lived. Jacob wanted Esau's inheritance. An inheritance was all the property and other things left to the oldest son when the father died. Jacob talked Esau into giving up his birthright for a bowl of lentil soup.

Q: Did Jacob try to trick Esau into giving up other things?

A: Jacob, with his mother's help, tricked Esau out of Isaac's blessing. This was even more valuable than the birthright. It could not be changed once it was given.

Q: What was the plan to get Isaac's blessing?

A: Rebekah overheard Isaac ask Esau to go hunt and bring back what he killed. Then Isaac would give Esau his blessing. Isaac was almost blind and Jacob pretended to be Esau by wearing Esau's clothes and by putting goatskins over his arms.

Q: What did Esau do when he lost Isaac's blessing?

A: Esau was furious! He begged Isaac for another blessing. But once a blessing was given another one couldn't be given. Rebekah heard that Esau might try to kill Jacob once Isaac died. She urged Isaac to send Jacob away. Isaac sent Jacob away.

LEAH

Q: Did Jacob get away safely and find a wife?

A: Jacob went to his uncle's home. Now it was Jacob's turn to be tricked. His Uncle Laban had two daughters, Leah and Rachel. Jacob loved Rachel. Laban agreed to let them marry if Jacob would work for seven years. Imagine Jacob's surprise when he discovered that his new bride was Leah!

RACHEL

Q: Did Jacob ever marry Rachel?

A: In those days a man could have several wives. So Jacob worked another seven years so he could marry Rachel. Jacob grew very rich. After many years Jacob packed up his wives, children, and flocks and returned to his home.

Q: Was Esau still angry with Jacob?

A: Jacob was afraid that Esau might still want to kill him. A messenger went ahead to talk with Esau. The messenger came back and said Esau was on his way to meet Jacob with 400 men. Jacob was frightened. However, Esau was so happy to see his brother again that he hugged him.

21

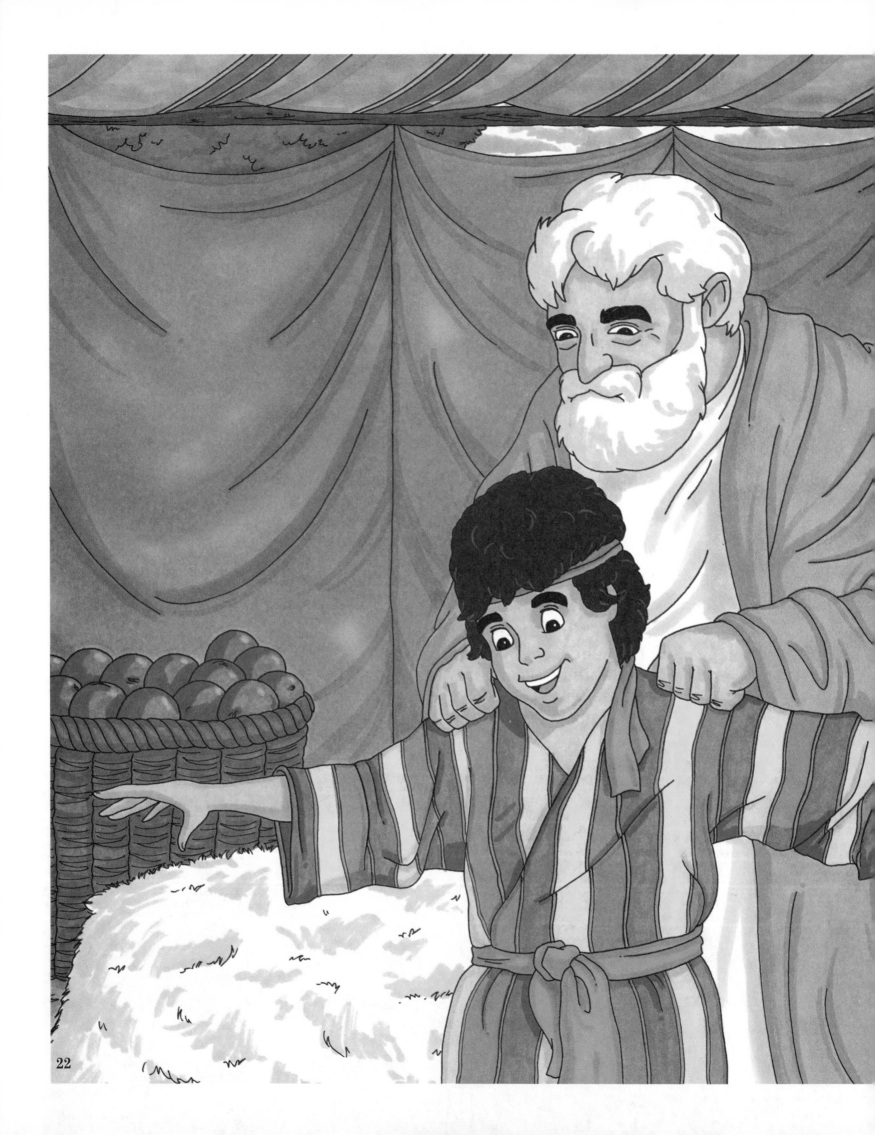

Q: What was Joseph's coat like?

A: The coat that Joseph's father, Jacob, gave him was long and had full sleeves. This was the kind of coat only important people wore. Joseph's older brothers were jealous.

Q: How did the brothers try to get back at Joseph?

A: They plotted to get rid of Joseph. They were also angry at Joseph's dreams. Joseph dreamed his brothers would all bow down to him. When Joseph came along, they threw him in a pit. The brothers wanted to kill Joseph, but one brother stopped them. Instead the brothers sold Joseph to be a slave in Egypt. They told their father, Jacob, that a wild animal had killed Joseph.

Q: Who bought Joseph?

A: Potiphar bought Joseph. But because Potiphar's wife lied about Joseph, he was thrown into jail.

Q: What happened to Joseph in jail?

A: Joseph was loyal to God and he tried to be useful. Everyone respected him. Joseph could tell what dreams meant.

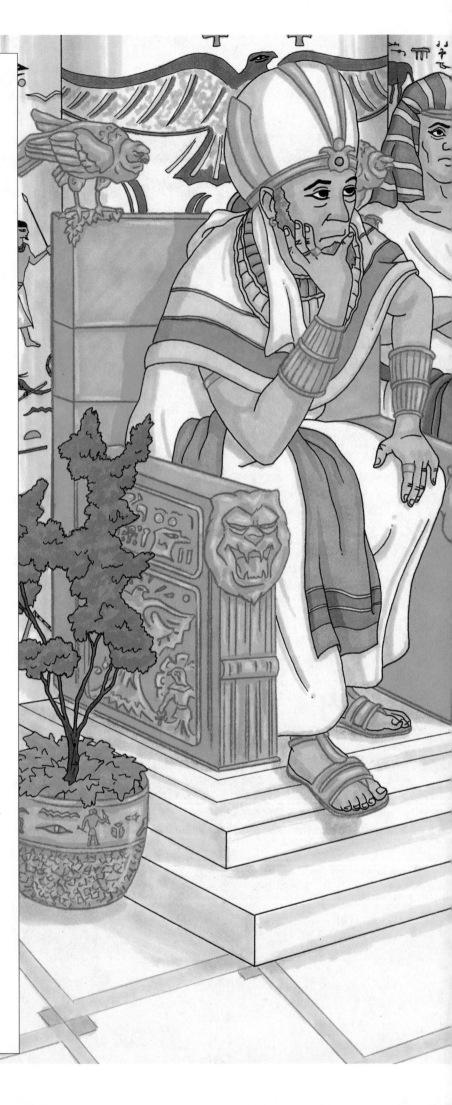

Q: How did telling about dreams help Joseph?

A: Pharaoh, the king of Egypt, had two strange dreams. Pharaoh had Joseph brought to him because Joseph could explain dreams.

Q: What were the king's dreams?

A: In his first dream, seven fat, healthy cows came out of the river. Then seven thin, bony cows came from the river and ate the fat cows. In the second dream, seven heads of ripe grain were growing on one stalk. Then seven dried-up heads of grain came up and ate the other. The dreams meant there would be seven years of good crops and then seven years of bad crops.

Q: Did the dreams come true?

A: Yes. The king followed Joseph's plan to save part of each good harvest. Because of this, there was plenty of food even for people from far away. Joseph's brothers went to Egypt for grain.

Q: Were the brothers surprised to see Joseph?

A: At first they did not recognize Joseph. Joseph finally told them who he was. He forgave his brothers.

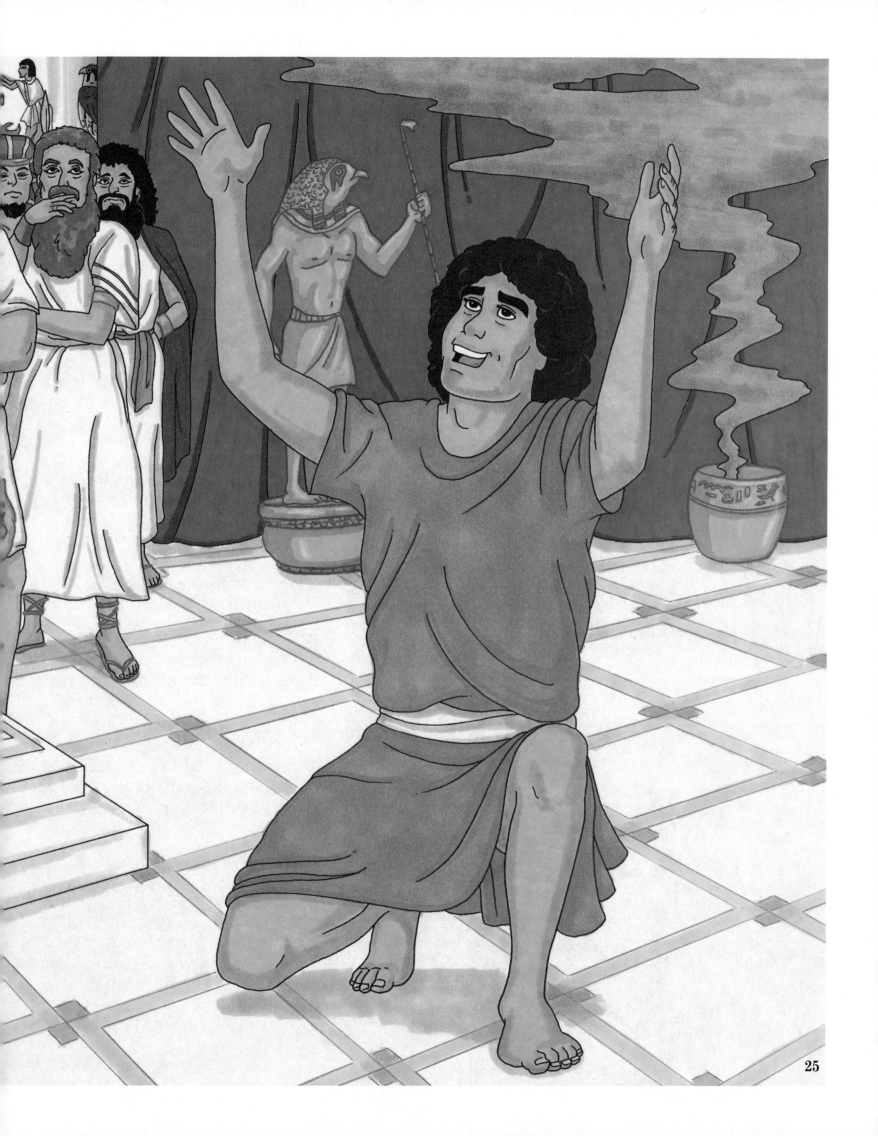

Q: Why was Moses in danger?

A: Four hundred years had passed since Joseph had helped the people of Egypt. There were so many Israelites in Egypt that Pharaoh was afraid they might turn against him, so he ordered the Israelites to work as slaves. Then he ordered the death of all Israelite baby boys.

Q: How did Moses' mother keep Moses alive?

A: After Moses was born his mother hid him. When he was three months old she made a little basket. She put Moses in the basket and gave it to Miriam, Moses' sister.

Q: Who found Moses?

A: Miriam went to the river. She set the basket near the reeds along the shore. She watched the basket float along. Pharaoh's daughter saw the basket and asked one of her maids to bring it to her. She opened the basket and knew it must be one of the Israelite babies.

Q: What did Pharaoh's daughter do with Moses?

A: She kept Moses as her son. When Moses was a young man he left Egypt because he did not like the way the Egyptians treated his people, the Israelites.

Q: What did Moses do when he saw a bush burning?

A: He stopped and looked, then turned to get a closer look. Moses must have thought it was very strange. The bush was on fire but it was not burning up! A voice came from the bush and told Moses to stop—this was holy ground. Moses stopped, took off his sandals, and covered his eyes.

Q: Who or what was the voice coming from the bush?

A: It was the voice of God. God told Moses his people in Egypt were suffering. They were slaves and they had prayed for God's help. They were ready to return to Canaan.

Q: What did God want Moses to do?

A: God told Moses to talk to Pharaoh and to the Israelites. It was time to take the Israelites out of Egypt. God warned Moses that Pharaoh would not listen at first. Once Pharaoh saw God's power, he would let the Israelites go.

Q: What did Moses tell God?

A: Moses argued with God. Moses was sure no one would believe that God sent him. Moses told God he didn't know how to speak so others would listen. God told Moses that he could do the job with God's help. Moses finally agreed to return to Egypt. His brother Aaron would do most of the talking.

27

Q: What is a plague?

A: A plague is harmful to many humans and animals. It must cover a large area and hurt most living things.

Q: Why were there so many plagues in Egypt?

A: God never sends a plague unless there is a good reason. God was using the plagues to get the Egyptians to let the Israelites leave.

Q: What were the ten plagues of Egypt?

A: First the water in the Nile River turned to blood. Next frogs overran the land. Then came gnats—tiny, biting, stinging insects. After the gnats, the flies came and next came a terrible disease. Then everyone got boils or nasty sores. After that, thunder and hail destroyed the land, locusts ate all the crops, and there were three days of darkness. Then Moses promised the worst plague— all the firstborn children would be killed.

Q: Did Pharaoh believe in God's power?

A: No. Pharaoh would not believe that God was more powerful than his magicians.

Q: How did Moses know what to do?

A: God spoke with Moses and told him what to do. Moses, with his brother Aaron's help, kept speaking for God. They showed God's power by bringing on more plagues. Pharaoh began to worry.

Q: What made Pharaoh finally change his mind?

A: Pharaoh changed his mind when his oldest son died, along with all the other firstborn sons in Egypt.

Q: Did the Israelite children die too?

A: No. Each family marked their door with the blood of a lamb. They roasted and ate the meat with bitter herbs and bread without yeast. The angel of death passed over the houses marked with blood.

Q: Did the Israelites finally leave Egypt?

A: Yes. The Egyptians wanted them to leave. They were tired of plagues and afraid of God. The Israelites asked the Egyptians for their gold and silver and it was given back to them. Their packing was done in a hurry. Soon they were on their way to the promised land.

29

Q: Did the Israelites have trouble traveling?

A: Yes. Pharaoh and his army chased after them to bring them back. In front of them was a huge sea and a huge pillar of cloud.

Q: What made the Israelites keep going?

A: God gave Moses amazing power. First the pillar of cloud blew over the people and hid them from the Egyptians. Then God told Moses to raise his walking stick high in the air. The water parted and the people crossed the sea on dry land.

Q: Didn't the Egyptians cross after them?

A: They tried. The horses galloped into the dry sea bed. The chariot wheels filled with sand. They all jumbled up together in the middle of the sea. Then God told Moses to spread his hand out over the dry sea. The waters came rushing back and the Egyptian soldiers all drowned.

Q: Did the Israelites celebrate?

A: They danced and sang and had a great celebration of thanksgiving. The Israelites were ready to believe in God and to trust Moses.

31

Q: Why did the Israelites wander for 40 years?

A: After living in Egypt many people no longer remembered how to worship God. Even though God always gave them what they needed, the people complained. It only took a short time to find the promised land, but God decided that they would have to go back into the wilderness. None of the people that complained would be allowed to live in the new land.

Q: What was the wilderness like?

A: It was a dry and rocky area with some mountains and deserts. The wilderness was very lonely and harsh.

Q: Did they ever want to go back to Egypt?

A: Yes. Every time they ran out of food or water, they got discouraged. It was hard for both people and animals. But God took care of them.

Q: How did God take care of them?

A: God always provided water and food. Every morning there was bread from heaven, *manna*. It must have looked funny because in Hebrew *manna* means "what is this stuff?"

Q: What are the Ten Commandments?

A: The Ten Commandments are rules to live by. The first four have to do with our relationship with God. The other six are rules for getting along with people. They are called commandments because they are rules from God.

Q: When did God give the commandments?

A: When the Israelites reached the wilderness of Sinai God asked Moses to get the people ready. They stayed near the base of a mountain called Mount Sinai and waited for a trumpet blast. The whole mountain shook when God spoke.

Q: What happened when God spoke?

A: The people were frightened. Moses told them that the Ten Commandments showed them what God wanted. Moses went up the mountain to talk with God. Moses was gone for 40 days. The Israelites forgot the commandments. They built a golden calf and worshiped it.

Q: Why was building an idol so bad?

A: The very first commandment says that no god is as important as the Lord God. The second warns against making an idol, which can be a statue of a god. Using God's name wrongly is the third commandment. Keeping the seventh day holy is the fourth. The people ignored God's wishes.

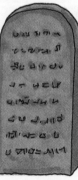

Q: What are the last six commandments?

A: The fifth commandment is about respecting your parents. The rest begin with "You shall not." These are: you shall not murder, you shall not be unfaithful to your husband or wife, you shall not steal, you shall not tell lies against your neighbor, and you shall not covet (strongly want) anything belonging to someone else.

Q: What happened when Moses came down from Mount Sinai?

A: When Moses saw the people worshiping an idol, he was very angry. He broke the stone tablets with the Ten Commandments. God was even more angry!

Q: How did God punish the people?

A: God said that those who disobeyed the commandments on purpose would not enter the promised land.

Q: How did the people remember the Ten Commandments?

A: God asked Moses to cut two stone tablets just like the first two. God would write the commandments on the tablets again. God really wanted the people to memorize them.

Q: Where was the promised land?

A: The land God promised to give to his people was west of the Jordan River. The Egyptians called it Canaan. It was northeast of Egypt, where the Israelites had lived for so long. The Mediterranean Sea was its western border. Today most of Israel is what was called the promised land.

Q: Why was it called the promised land?

A: God made a covenant with Abraham. If Abraham would accept God as his Lord, then God would give him Canaan. A covenant is a promise, so Canaan became the promised land.

Q: What was the promised land like?

A: It was often called the land of milk and honey. This means the land was good for flocks (where they got milk) and for farmers (honey comes from the land). Many crops grew along the streams leading to the Jordan River. There was plenty of grass to feed the flocks.

Q: Was Moses still in charge when they got to Canaan?

A: Moses was old. He had led the people for 40 years. When the Israelites reached the Jordan River, Moses stood on a hill and looked out at the promised land. God did not give Moses permission to enter the land with his people.

Q: Who would lead the people after Moses?

A: Moses named Joshua the new leader. The people promised to follow Joshua and to obey the laws Moses had taught them. Joshua was a good military leader.

Q: Didn't God promise to give them the land?

A: He assured Joshua that although they might need to go to war, the land would be theirs. As long as they remained loyal to God, everything would go well for them.

Q: Did the Israelites just walk into the promised land?

A: Before they crossed the Jordan River into the promised land, they had some important jobs to do. They needed to get ready to fight. Joshua needed to find out all he could about the nearby land and about the closest city of Jericho. Joshua ordered the fighting men to get ready. Then he sent two spies to Jericho.

Q: What happened to the spies?

A: The spies looked around, then went to the house of Rahab, a woman who wanted to obey God. The king of Jericho heard that Israelite spies were in the city. Rahab hid the men under some reeds on the roof of her house. She gave them a way to escape and the spies promised to protect her and her family. Although soldiers of Jericho looked everywhere they didn't find the spies.

Q: How did the battle of Jericho start?

A: It wasn't like the wars we have today. It didn't start with two armies fighting. God wanted the priests to lead the way with the Ark of God.

Q: What was the Ark of God?

A: It was a decorated box that the Israelites carried precious things in. In it were the Ten Commandments, a pot of manna, and Aaron's walking staff. God wanted them to carry the Ark in front because this was a sign to everyone that God was with his people. When the people of Jericho saw the priests, the Ark, and the thousands of Israelites, they were scared.

Q: How did the Israelites get in the city?

A: Every day for six days the warriors walked around the city. Seven priests carried trumpets and went in front of the Ark. On the seventh day they walked around the city seven times, with the priests blowing on their trumpets. When the trumpets sounded the people shouted as loudly as they could, then the walls of Jericho crumbled and fell. All the people of Jericho, except Rahab and her family, were killed.

Q: Was Deborah like the judges we have today?

A: Although Deborah sometimes settled arguments and gave advice, she did not work as judges do today. Her courtroom was under a palm tree, where the people came to her for help. She was also a prophet; that is a person who speaks for God. She could also lead in battle as a soldier.

Q: What kind of military advice did she give?

A: She had a plan to defeat Sisera, the commander of the enemy king's army. Deborah spoke for God and asked Barak to bring 10,000 men. She would show him how to get rid of Sisera and his army.

Q: Why did she want to get rid of Sisera?

A: The people of Israel were having trouble with their neighbors. The Syrians weren't happy that the Israelites had moved into their land. Sisera was the general who bothered them the most.

Q: How did Deborah beat Sisera's army?

A: Deborah went with Barak and the army. Deborah told Barak that God was with them and the army. With Deborah beside him, Barak set out with his troops. When Sisera and his army saw all the soldiers coming, they got scared and ran every which way. Barak and Deborah won the battle.

Q: What was Samson famous for?

A: Samson was amazingly strong. Once he tore a young lion apart with his bare hands. Another time he killed 30 men by himself.

Q: What made Samson so strong?

A: His strength was in his hair. Samson's mother had been warned never to cut it nor let anyone else cut it. Samson's long hair was a sign that he was a special person to God.

Q: Why did Israel need a hero like Samson?

A: The Bible says that the Israelites were again sinful. This angered God. So God let their neighbors, the Philistines, overpower them. When God's people prayed for help, God decided to send someone to help them. God gave Samson special powers so he could defeat the Philistines.

Q: What kind of enemy were the Philistines?

A: The Philistines had good armies. They were also tricky—they could not be trusted. Most likely they were bullies. Even worse, they did not believe in or respect God.

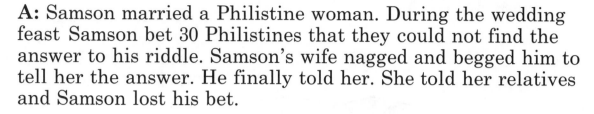

Q: How did Samson get to know the Philistines?

A: Samson married a Philistine woman. During the wedding feast Samson bet 30 Philistines that they could not find the answer to his riddle. Samson's wife nagged and begged him to tell her the answer. He finally told her. She told her relatives and Samson lost his bet.

Q: How did Samson pay off his bet?

A: Samson was very angry. He paid off the bet by killing 30 men and giving their best wedding clothes to his wife's family. Samson left his wife and went back to his parents' house. Samson used his strength over and over again. Then Samson fell in love with a woman named Delilah.

Q: What did Delilah do to Samson?

A: Some Philistine leaders asked Delilah to find out where Samson got his strength. Each night Samson told her a different story. None of the stories were true and Delilah grew frustrated. Finally Samson told her that his strength was in his hair. Delilah had a man cut Samson's hair while he slept.

Q: Did Samson lose his strength after his hair was cut?

A: Yes. The Philistines grabbed him and put out his eyes. They put him to work in a mill. However, as Samson's hair grew, so did his strength. At a great Philistine celebration they wanted Samson to entertain them. But Samson was strong again. He pushed on the pillars holding up the building. The building crashed down and Samson and the Philistines were killed.

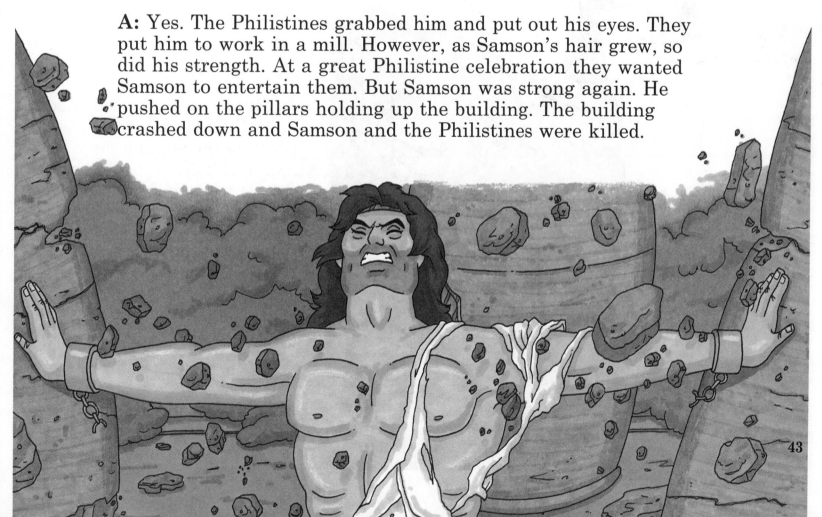

Q: Who was Naomi?

A: Naomi was from Bethlehem, but moved to the country of Moab with her husband and two sons. Her two sons married Moabite women, Ruth and Orpah. When Naomi's husband died she went to live with her sons, but they also died. In Bible times a widow was cared for by her children or by her husband's family. Naomi had no one to care for her in Moab. So Naomi decided to return to Bethlehem.

Q: Why would it be better for Naomi in Bethlehem?

A: Although she had no close relatives, a relative of her husband's lived in Bethlehem. His name was Boaz and he was rich and successful.

Q: Did Naomi go to Bethlehem alone?

A: Ruth and Orpah decided to go with Naomi. They loved their mother-in-law very much. But Naomi told them to return to their fathers' homes. Orpah decided to stay in Moab, but Ruth would not leave Naomi.

Q: Why didn't they get jobs and stay together?

A: Bible women didn't have the kind of jobs women have today. Women could only work in the home.

Q: What did Ruth and Naomi do?

A: Ruth and Naomi went to the town of Bethlehem. It was harvest time when they got there. Ruth went to pick up grain left in the fields after the harvest. She hoped someone would notice her. Ruth wanted to marry again.

Q: Did Ruth meet someone special?

A: The people who were harvesting grain were curious about Ruth. Boaz came along to the field he owned. He saw Ruth picking up grain. Boaz asked who she was. When he was told that she was the Moabite who had come with Naomi, he went to talk to her.

Q: What did Boaz want to talk to Ruth about?

A: Boaz felt responsible for Ruth since Naomi was his relative. He showed Ruth where the best grain was. Boaz invited her to help herself to water and to stay with the women where she would be safe. Naomi thought Boaz would be a good husband for Ruth.

Q: Did Boaz and Ruth get married?

A: Yes. Then Ruth and Boaz had a baby boy, Obed, and Naomi helped care for him.

Q: What was unusual about Samuel's birth?

A: Samuel was born to Hannah, who could have no children.

Q: Why was having a child so important?

A: A child was a special blessing from God. Children grew up and took care of their parents. Having children meant that some part of you lived forever.

Q: How was it that Samuel was finally born?

A: Hannah prayed to God in the temple at Shiloh. She promised that if she had a son she would give him to the Lord. Eli the priest watched her and wondered if she were drunk because her lips were moving in silent prayer. He asked her to leave. When Hannah explained that she was praying for a son, Eli told her that her prayers would be answered. Later Samuel was born.

Q: What did it mean to give Samuel to the Lord?

A: It meant that Samuel would be trained to be a priest. When he was two, Hannah took Samuel to Eli. Hannah left Samuel there and went home. Hannah kept her promise to God.

Q: Why did Samuel choose David to be the king?

A: Samuel was very important in Israel. People went to him for advice and help. Samuel was also a prophet. God used Samuel to tell the people what God wanted. Samuel anointed David king because God told him to.

Q: What does anoint mean?

A: Anoint usually means to put perfumed oil on a person's head or body. When a king was anointed, that king became a servant of God.

Q: How did Samuel find David?

A: God told Samuel to go to Bethlehem and look for a man named Jesse. God wanted one of his sons to be the next king of Israel. Samuel looked at each son carefully. But God didn't want any of the seven sons that Samuel saw to be king of Israel.

Q: How did Samuel find the king?

A: Samuel asked Jesse if he had any more sons. Jesse said his youngest son, David, was with the sheep. Samuel asked him to send for David. God told Samuel that David was to be the next king. Samuel anointed David. David knew God was with him.

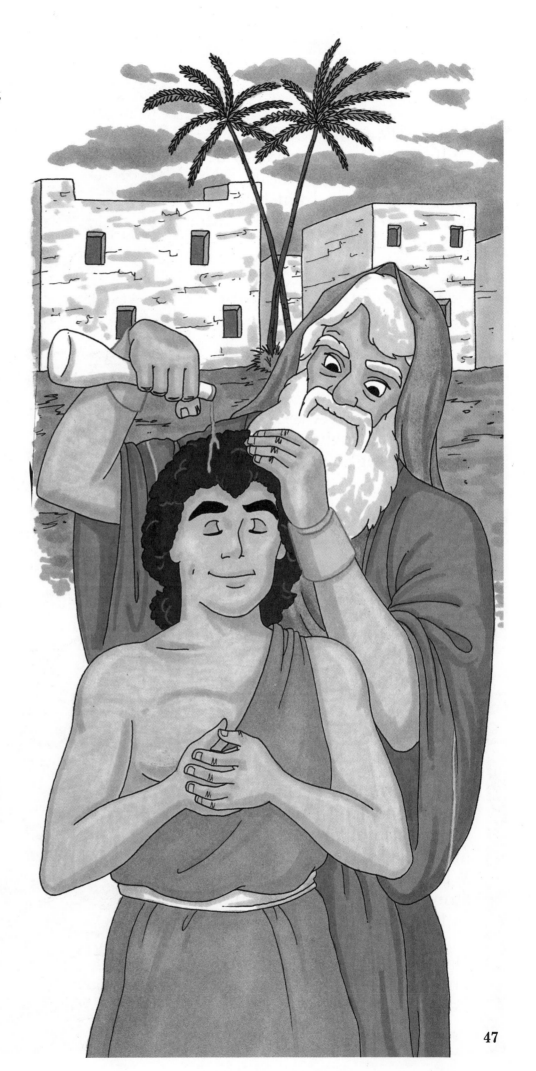

47

Q: Why did David and Goliath fight?

A: David's people and Goliath's people were at war. Goliath challenged Israel to send someone to fight him, but no one wanted to. Goliath was over nine feet tall!

Q: How did David get into the fight with Goliath?

A: Three of David's brothers were with the army. Their father sent David to take food to his brothers. After David heard Goliath shouting, he offered to fight.

Q: How did David talk the king into letting him fight?

A: David told how he had often killed lions and bears. Also, David knew that God was with him. David went to face Goliath with only his sling and five smooth stones.

Q: How could a sling and some stones kill a giant?

A: The sling was a leather pouch that had leather thongs. David swung it around and around his head. With a flick of his wrist, the stone zoomed and hit Goliath in the middle of the forehead. The giant fell face down. David took Goliath's sword and chopped off the giant's head!

Q: What was David the king of?

A: David was king of the whole land of Israel. He was able to bring together all of God's people in the promised land. David was a clever general and a popular leader, but he had many enemies. He was only 30 years old when he became king.

Q: What city did David choose for his capital?

A: Jerusalem was in the center of the country on the border between two important tribes. David thought it would make a fine capital, but the Jebusites held the city. David sneaked his soldiers into the city through a water tunnel. They were quickly inside the walls. Then it was easy to take over Jerusalem.

Q: Did David always please God when he was king?

A: No. One time David fell in love with another man's wife. He had the husband killed so he could marry the woman. That woman was Bathsheba, who was the mother of Solomon. But David always asked God's forgiveness. He truly loved God. David often wrote songs of praise to God, some of which are in the book of Psalms.

Q: Why did David choose Solomon as the next king?

A: David's son Adonijah was the oldest living prince. He was so sure he would be named king that he invited some of his brothers and friends to a celebration. But Bathsheba talked David into choosing Solomon.

Q: What did Adonijah think of Solomon becoming king?

A: When Solomon rode into the city on his father's mule, the crowds started cheering. Adonijah heard the uproar. When he learned that his half brother Solomon was anointed king, he was very frightened. Perhaps Solomon would be angry that he had named himself king first.

Q: Did Solomon hurt Adonijah?

A: No. Solomon forgave Adonijah and said no one was to harm a hair on his head. As long as Adonijah remained loyal to Solomon, nothing would hurt him.

Q: Was David still alive when Solomon became king?

A: Yes, but he was very old. He called Solomon to his bedside. First he told Solomon to follow in the ways of the Lord. Next he told Solomon to have courage and to use wisdom in ruling the people. After that David died.

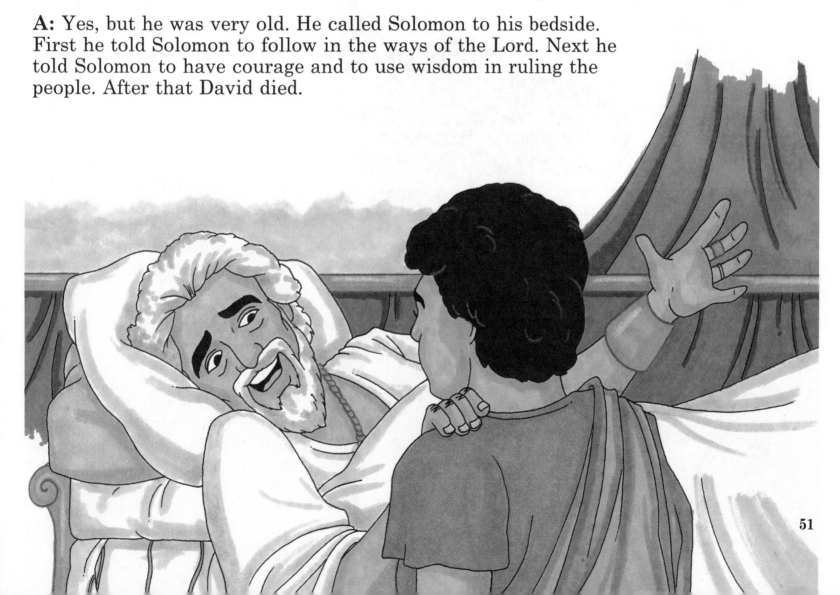

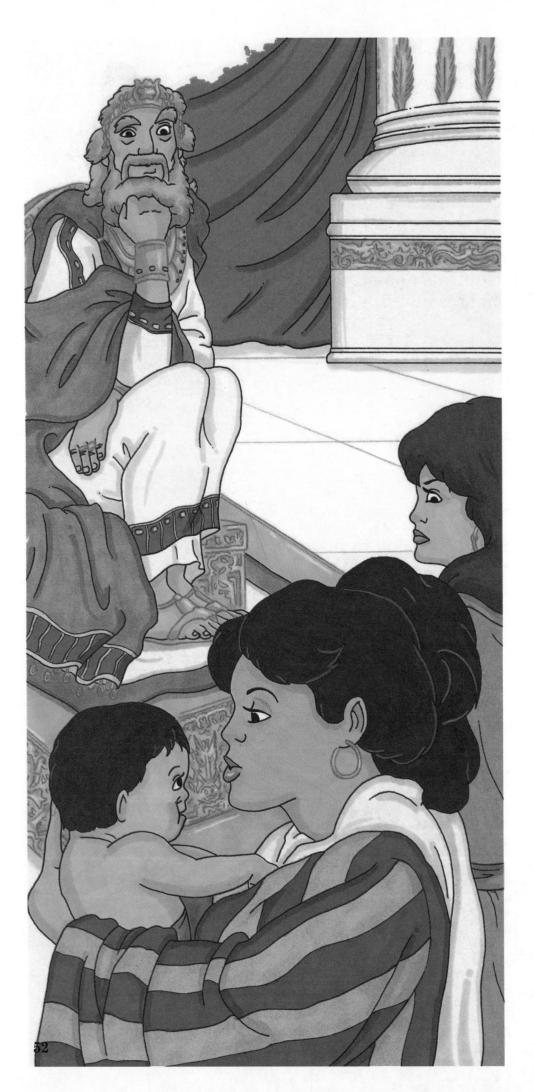

Q: Was Solomon the smartest man?

A: He may have been smarter than other people. But wisdom is something more than intelligence. Solomon had common sense. Solomon prayed that God would help him make wise decisions.

Q: What was something wise that Solomon did?

A: Two women came to King Solomon. They had a baby with them. Both women said the child was theirs. Each accused the other of stealing her baby and putting a dead baby in its place.

Q: How did Solomon decide who was the real mother?

A: He ordered that the child be cut in half and said that each woman would get half. The real mother said to give the living boy to the other woman—she did not want the child killed. When he heard her words, he gave her the child. He knew that the real mother would not allow the baby to be harmed.

Q: What other wise things did Solomon do?

A: Solomon was a careful trader and merchant. He had a beautiful temple to God built, and a palace for himself, while keeping peace in the land.

Q: What are proverbs?

A: Proverbs are written by wise people like Solomon—they are not rules from God. The wise sayings of Solomon were used to teach people how to behave.

Q: Did Solomon use his wisdom in his job as king?

A: Yes. Solomon must have been a wise ruler because people from other countries heard about him. Many people came to visit Solomon and see the beautiful temple he had built. Some visitors wanted to match wits with him.

Q: Who were some of Solomon's visitors?

A: The queen of Sheba heard about Solomon and decided to visit. She had many questions and wanted to see what advice he would offer. The queen also wanted to test Solomon to see if he was wise. She came to Jerusalem with lots of servants and with camels loaded with gold, spices, and jewels.

Q: What did the queen of Sheba think of Solomon?

A: The queen talked a long time with Solomon. She asked very hard questions. When they were finished the queen was surprised. Solomon had more wisdom than she expected.

Q: What did Elijah do?

A: Elijah tried to convince the people of Israel and their king, Ahab, to worship only God. The main god of the Canaanite people was called Baal. When the Israelites settled in Canaan, they sometimes worshiped both Baal and God.

Q: What was Baal like?

A: People thought Baal was a nature god, but he wasn't a god at all. He was make-believe. The people thought he brought good crops and large harvests. They built statues of Baal and made sacrifices to him.

Q: How did Elijah change people's minds?

A: Elijah called for a contest between God and Baal. If the people could see how powerful God was, maybe they would stop worshiping Baal. Elijah asked the 450 prophets of Baal and the 400 prophets of other gods to meet him on Mount Carmel.

Q: What happened when they got to Mount Carmel?

A: Elijah dared the people to choose. They could follow God or Baal; but they could not do both. He called for two bulls for a sacrifice. Elijah and the prophets would each cut up their bull and put it on a stack of wood on the altar.

Q: What was the contest between Elijah and the prophets?

A: Elijah told the prophets to call on their god to send fire to burn the sacrifice. Then Elijah would do the same. Whichever god answered by sending fire would be the winner.

Q: How did the prophets try to get Baal to send fire?

A: They danced and they prayed. Around the altar they cried out, "O Baal, answer us!" By noon there was still no fire. Elijah teased them. The prophets danced harder until Elijah stopped them.

Q: How did Elijah prove there is only one God?

A: He dug a trench around his altar. Elijah poured water over the offering until it was soaked and the trench was full of water. Then he asked God to show the people that the God of Israel was the true Lord. The fire came down and burned everything, even the dust on the ground. Then the people grabbed the prophets of Baal and Elijah killed them all. They had learned who the real God is!

Q: How did Elijah die?

A: He didn't really die. Instead, a chariot of fire and horses of fire came down and Elijah went up to heaven in a whirlwind.

Q: What did the big fish have to do with Jonah?

A: The fish was Jonah's transportation to Nineveh. God asked Jonah to go to Nineveh and warn the people. Jonah didn't want to. He got on a boat going in the opposite direction. Jonah thought he could get away from God.

Q: What did God do about Jonah?

A: God sent a great wind and storm that terrified the sailors on Jonah's boat. They prayed to their gods and even threw some of the cargo overboard. Nothing worked! The sailors woke up Jonah and asked him to pray to his god.

Q: What did the sailors believe about the storm?

A: They were sure that god was angry and sent the storm. The sailors asked Jonah who he was and who his god was. When Jonah told them he worshiped the Lord, the sailors were more frightened than ever. Jonah's God must be very powerful!

Q: What did Jonah tell the sailors to do?

A: Jonah told the sailors to throw him overboard. The sailors didn't want to do this. But the storm only got worse.

56

Q: Did the storm let up?

A: Not until the sailors tossed Jonah into the sea. Then the water calmed down. God sent a great fish to swallow Jonah. Jonah knew he should have obeyed God.

Q: How did Jonah get out of the big fish?

A: The fish spit him out on the beach not far from Nineveh. This is where he should have gone to begin with! God told him to give Nineveh a warning.

Q: Did Jonah obey God this time?

A: Jonah did what he was told. The people of Nineveh believed the message Jonah brought. God forgave the people and did not destroy the city. Jonah went to a hill where he could watch Nineveh. He was mad at God and hoped God might change his mind and destroy the city.

Q: Did God change his mind?

A: God did not change his mind about Nineveh. God had a plant grow for shade for Jonah. Then God made the plant die. Jonah was mad. But God told him that if he cared for the plant then God must care even more about the people of Nineveh.

58

Q: Who were Shadrach, Meshach, and Abednego?

A: They were three young Israelites who were put in King Nebuchadnezzar's palace. Daniel was also in the king's palace.

Q: Why did the king throw the boys into a furnace?

A: The young men refused to worship a huge statue. All the leaders of the land were called to Babylon to worship the statue. Daniel's friends would not obey the king's order. Nebuchadnezzar was so angry his face turned red. He ordered the young men to be tossed into a furnace seven times hotter than usual.

Q: Why did they risk their lives in the furnace?

A: Shadrach, Meshach, and Abednego worshiped only God. If they bowed down to the statue they would be breaking God's commandments.

Q: Did the young men burn in the furnace?

A: Their clothes were not burned and not a hair on their heads was hurt. The king was astonished! When he looked in the furnace he saw four men. Who was the fourth? Could it have been an angel of God?

Q: What was Daniel doing in a lions' den?

A: King Darius ordered him in there. Some of the leaders of the country passed a law that said you could not pray to God. Daniel disobeyed because he loved God.

Q: Why was there a plot against Daniel?

A: The leaders in Babylon were jealous of Daniel. Daniel was so honest and capable that the king gave him power.

Q: What law did Daniel disobey?

A: The law said that for 30 days people could only pray to King Darius. But Daniel went to his room three times a day to praise God and pray. The leaders spied on Daniel, saw him praying, and told the king. The unhappy king tried all day to save Daniel from the lions' den.

Q: What happened to Daniel in the den of lions?

A: The king told Daniel that he hoped his God would protect him. The next morning the king hurried to the den. He called out to Daniel. When Daniel answered, the king was overjoyed! God had sent an angel to shut the lions' mouths.

Q: Who was Queen Esther?

A: Esther was a pretty, clever Jewish girl who saved her people. King Ahasuerus thought she was so lovely that he made her his queen.

Q: Why did Haman want to get rid of the Jews?

A: Haman was very proud. He expected everyone to bow down to him. Esther's uncle, Mordecai, would only bow to God. Because he hated Mordecai, Haman talked the king into killing all the Jews.

Q: How did Esther save her people?

A: She dressed in her finest clothes and planned a banquet. She invited the king and Haman. The king was so pleased he offered Esther whatever she wanted. Esther told him how an evil man planned to kill her people. She asked the king to change the order. When the king learned Haman was the man, he was angry!

Q: What happened to Haman?

A: The king tricked Haman into honoring Mordecai. Haman had built gallows so that he could hang Mordecai, but instead the king had Haman hanged.

BIBLE PEOPLE

Q: Who was Job?

A: Job was a very rich man. He had a lot of silver and gold, and many sheep, oxen, camels, and donkeys. He also had a very large family. Everyone admired him. Job loved and trusted God. But Satan did not like Job.

Q: What did Satan do to Job?

A: God told Satan that Job was a good man. Satan told God that the only reason that Job was good was because God had made him wealthy. God knew that Job would remain faithful even if he did not have riches. Satan took away all of Job's wealth and his family. Job still trusted God and followed him. Satan was angry.

Q: Did Satan stop hurting Job?

A: No. Satan told God that if Job were to lose his health he would not be faithful. Satan then took away Job's health. Job was covered with sores from his head to his feet. He became very sick.

Q: What happened to Job?

A: Even though Job was very sick, he did not curse God. He still loved God. God told Satan not to bother Job any more. Then God gave Job back his wealth—he was twice as rich as before. God also gave Job more children.

Q: Who were the Israelites?

A: The Israelites were descendants of Abraham. Abraham had a son named Isaac. Isaac had a son named Jacob. Jacob had twelve sons and from them came the twelve tribes of Israel.

Q: Do the Israelites have any other names?

A: Yes. Sometimes they are called the children of Israel or the people of Israel. They are also called God's chosen people.

Q: Why does the Bible tell the stories of the people of Israel?

A: God uses the people of Israel to show how he loves humankind. Even though the people of Israel did not always do what was right, God always loved them and forgave them.

Q: What can we learn from Israel's disobedience?

A: When Israel disobeyed God, they always got into trouble. When they obeyed God, there was always a blessing. Doing right brings happiness. Doing wrong brings unhappiness. Either way, however, God's love for his people never goes away.

Q: What kind of religion did the Egyptians have?

A: The Egyptians believed in many different gods. They did not obey the God of Israel. The Egyptians believed that when people died, they would live again in another life. They built great tombs and filled them with gold, food, and goods. They thought these things would be used by the dead in another world.

Q: Were the Egyptians the enemies of the Israelites?

A: Sometimes. Abraham and Jacob went to Egypt because it had food when their land did not. Joseph was a famous Israelite who helped the pharaoh (king) of the Egyptians. But the Egyptians made the people of Israel slaves hundreds of years after Joseph. God sent Moses to rescue the people of Israel from slavery.

Q: How did Joseph meet the Egyptians?

A: Joseph was sold by his brothers into slavery to the Egyptians. Later Joseph interpreted a dream for the Egyptian pharaoh. The pharaoh was so pleased that he made Joseph his second in command. Joseph was then able to help his family during a famine and move to the land of Egypt.

Q: Who was Gideon?

A: God told Gideon that he was to be the leader of Israel. Gideon did not want the job. He asked God to give him a sign that he should be the leader. God gave Gideon a sign by keeping a fleece dry when the ground was wet.

Q: Why did the people of Israel need a leader?

A: When the people of Israel stopped following God, their enemies conquered them. The people of Israel were ruled by foreign kings.

Q: What did Gideon do?

A: Gideon gathered a large army, but God told him he had too many men. Gideon sent the frightened soldiers home. God told Gideon that he still had too many men. Gideon kept only 300 men.

Q: How did such a small army conquer a large army?

A: Gideon's army took torches and clay pots and sneaked up on the enemy's army at night. They surrounded the large army and broke the clay pots at the same time and yelled. The enemy thought Gideon's army was much bigger. They ran for their lives. Gideon won a great victory.

Q: Who was the first person to play the harp?

A: Jubal was the first person to play the harp. Cain, Adam and Eve's son, was one of his ancestors. Because Jubal was the first to play it, we say Jubal is the father of those who play stringed instruments.

Q: Who was the most famous harp player?

A: David, the son of Jesse, was a very good harp player. He was also a great warrior, who later became king of Israel.

Q: Who played the cymbals?

A: King David had men who would play musical instruments before the Lord. Asaph, who was in charge of the musicians, played the loud-sounding cymbals. Benaiah and Jahaziel blew the trumpets, and others played harps and lyres.

Q: Who hung their harps in the willow bushes?

A: The people of Israel were so sad when they lived in Babylon that they could not play their harps, so they hung them on the willows. They remembered their home in Israel and wept.

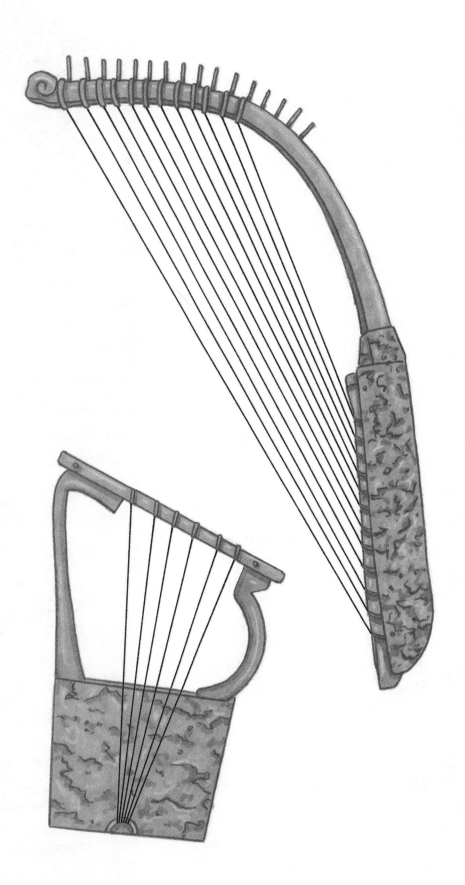

Q: Who was Balak?

A: Balak was the king of the Moabites. He was afraid of the Israelites—he did not want them to live in his land east of the River Jordan.

Q: Who was Balaam?

A: Balaam was a very wise man. King Balak asked Balaam to put a curse on the Israelites. He told Balaam that he would give him gold to do this. God spoke to Balaam and told him to give Israel a blessing, not a curse. Balak sent more gold to Balaam to get him to say the curse.

Q: What happened to Balaam on his journey?

A: Balaam got on his donkey and rode down the road. Suddenly his donkey would not go forward. The donkey had seen an angel standing in the way. This happened several times. Finally the donkey spoke and told Balaam not to beat him. Balaam's eyes were opened and he also saw the angel.

Q: Did Balaam ever curse the Israelites?

A: No. Balaam could not curse the Israelites. Even though King Balak offered him a lot of money, Balaam did not disobey God.

Q: Where did the Philistines come from?

A: Some people think the Philistines came from Greece or Turkey. In Bible times they moved to the west coast of Canaan.

Q: What made the Philistines great?

A: The Philistines were more advanced than most of their neighbors. They knew more about metal working, which helped them make weapons and farming tools. They also knew more about farming. They were a very wealthy nation and had many chariots.

Q: Who was the person who gave the Philistines trouble?

A: The Philistines were enemies of the people of Israel. An Israelite named Samson destroyed many Philistines with his great strength.

Q: What famous Israelite king went to war with the Philistines?

A: The man was King David. King David had many battles with the Philistines, and he won many victories. David is most famous for his battle with the giant Goliath, when the Philistines wanted to attack Israel.

Q: Who were the Assyrians?

A: The Assyrians had a very great empire. They lived in the area that is today called northern Iraq. They were enemies of the people of Israel.

Q: What did the angel of the Lord do to the Assyrians?

A: The Assyrians attacked Jerusalem. They wanted to have a war with King Hezekiah. The king was afraid and prayed to God. God answered Hezekiah's prayer. God helped the people of Jerusalem by sending the angel of the Lord. The angel went to the Assyrian camp and many Assyrian soldiers died. The people of Jerusalem were rescued.

Q: What famous city was an Assyrian city?

A: The most famous Assyrian city was Nineveh. God told Jonah to go to Nineveh and tell the Assyrians to turn from their wicked ways and repent. If they would not, God would destroy them. Jonah did not want to take the message to these cruel people, but he finally went to Nineveh.

Q: What happened after the Assyrians heard Jonah's message?

A: All the people of the city were afraid. They prayed and asked God to forgive them. God did not punish the people because they believed Jonah. The people of Nineveh started doing good.

Q: Who wore a disguise and visited a witch?

A: King Saul did. He was about to go to war with the Philistines, his enemies. He was afraid and asked God what to do, but God did not answer. Saul then put on a disguise to visit a witch. He hoped she might tell him what to do. She made Samuel the prophet appear, who told Saul that he would lose the battle and die.

Q: Who was killed when he wore a disguise?

A: King Josiah wanted to go to battle with Neco, the king of Egypt. God told him not to. Josiah put on a disguise and went to war anyway. The archers shot King Josiah, and he later died.

Q: Who wore a disguise to fool King David?

A: Joab, King David's servant, wanted to save the life of Absalom, David's son. Joab asked a woman to disguise herself as a mourner and go to King David with a message. The woman's message helped save Absalom's life. King David discovered the disguise, but he did not punish the woman or Joab.

Q: Who escaped by putting an idol in his bed?

A: King Saul was trying to kill David. Michal, David's wife, helped him escape from Saul. She put a large idol in David's bed. She put goat's hair on the idol's head and covered it with clothes. This fooled the soldiers long enough for David to escape.

Q: Who escaped by hiding in a well?

A: Two of David's men heard about Absalom's plot against David. They were going to tell David, but Absalom's men were searching for David's men. So David's men hid in a well and a woman covered the well with a cloth and sprinkled grain over it. Absalom's men did not find them. They later escaped and told David of the plot.

Q: Who escaped by riding a horse?

A: King Benhadad surrounded the city of Samaria and planned to attack it. The king of Samaria was afraid, but God told him that he would win the battle. The king of Samaria sent the young men out of the city and they won a great victory. King Benhadad escaped by riding away on a horse.

Q: What warrior commanded the sun to stand still?

A: The Gibeonites had made a peace treaty with Israel. They sent a message to Joshua that the Amorites were attacking them. Joshua and his army marched all night to rescue them. Joshua asked the Lord to make the sun stand still so that they would have more time for the battle.

Q: Who was the warrior that covered the ground with salt?

A: King Abimelech was a very wicked man. When he attacked the city of Shechem he killed many people. He then put salt over the ground so that no one could grow any crops.

Q: Who was the Israelite woman who led thousands in battle?

A: Deborah was a judge over Israel in the years after Joshua. She led 10,000 soldiers in a courageous battle against the Syrian army.

Q: Who was the warrior that was given a bride?

A: Caleb said he would give his daughter in marriage to anyone who would conquer the town of Debir. Othniel won the battle. Caleb gave Achsah, his daughter, to be Othniel's wife.

Q: What was Abishai famous for?

A: Abishai was one of King David's famous warriors. He was in a battle where he killed 300 men by himself. He was one of the most important of David's mighty men.

Q: Who brought water for King David to drink?

A: Three of David's mighty men were in the cave of Adullam. They heard David whisper to himself that he would like to have a drink from the well at Bethlehem. The three sneaked past the enemy and went on a 30 mile trip to get David the water.

Q: Who were expert archers and slingers?

A: There were 700 men from the tribe of Benjamin who joined King David's mighty men. They could shoot a bow and arrow equally well with the right or left hand. They could also throw a sling shot with either the right or left hand.

Q: Who could run as fast as deer?

A: The men from the tribe of Gad joined King David's mighty men in the wilderness. They were experts with the shield and spear. They could run as fast as deer.

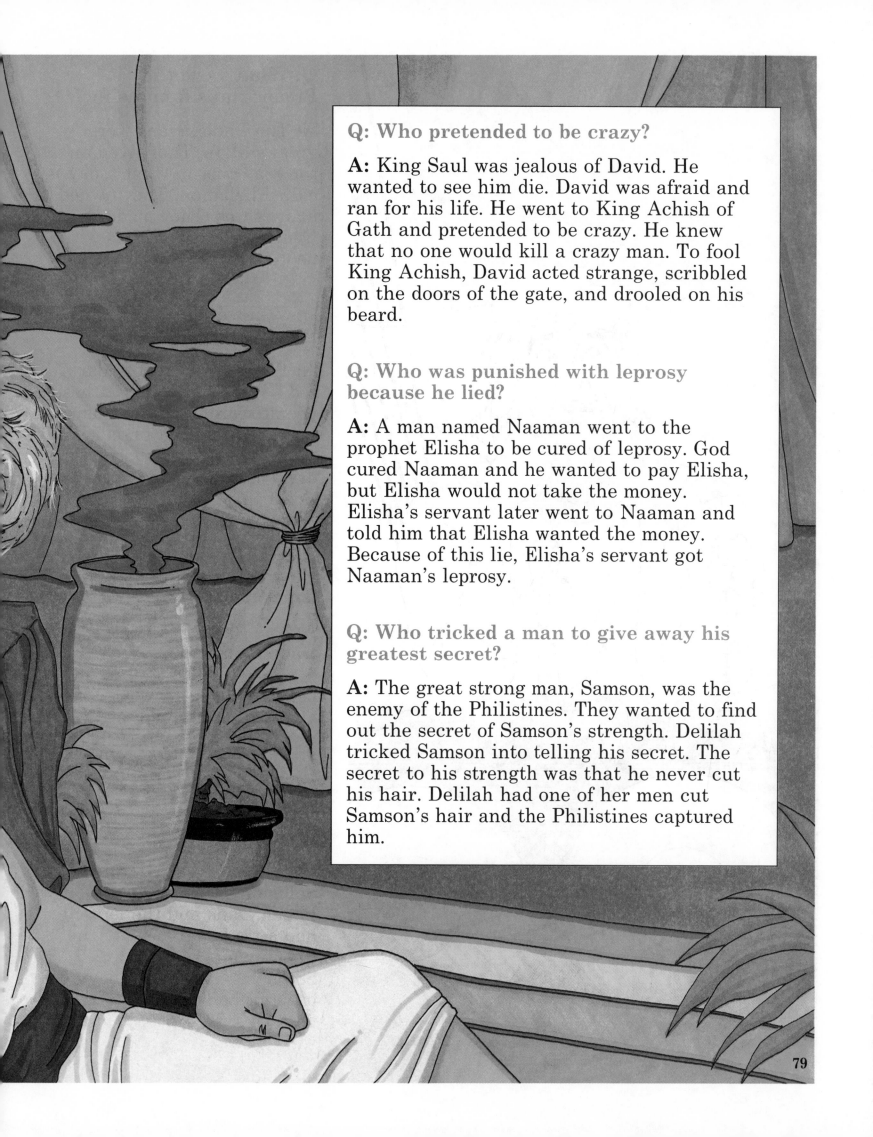

Q: Who pretended to be crazy?

A: King Saul was jealous of David. He wanted to see him die. David was afraid and ran for his life. He went to King Achish of Gath and pretended to be crazy. He knew that no one would kill a crazy man. To fool King Achish, David acted strange, scribbled on the doors of the gate, and drooled on his beard.

Q: Who was punished with leprosy because he lied?

A: A man named Naaman went to the prophet Elisha to be cured of leprosy. God cured Naaman and he wanted to pay Elisha, but Elisha would not take the money. Elisha's servant later went to Naaman and told him that Elisha wanted the money. Because of this lie, Elisha's servant got Naaman's leprosy.

Q: Who tricked a man to give away his greatest secret?

A: The great strong man, Samson, was the enemy of the Philistines. They wanted to find out the secret of Samson's strength. Delilah tricked Samson into telling his secret. The secret to his strength was that he never cut his hair. Delilah had one of her men cut Samson's hair and the Philistines captured him.

Q: What were the Phoenicians famous for?

A: The Phoenicians were great sailors. They lived on the sea coast in what today is called Lebanon. They owned many ships. They made their living by trading goods with people from other lands.

Q: What does the name Phoenician mean?

A: Phoenician means "dark red." It is believed that these people were given that name because of a crimson-purple dye that they discovered. The dye was made from a type of shellfish.

Q: Where did the Phoenicians sail their boats?

A: The Phoenicians had trading posts on the African coast. They also traded with people from Cyprus, Greece, Spain, and Sicily.

Q: What famous person used their ships?

A: King David made an agreement with the King of Tyre. Later, during King Solomon's time, the Phoenicians and the Israelites had a trade agreement. The Phoenicians sailed King Solomon's ships and they brought back ivory, apes, and peacocks.

Q: Who were the Hittites?

A: The Hittites came from one of Noah's sons, Ham. They were a great nation that had an important empire in what we today call Turkey.

Q: What happened between the Hittites and the people of Israel?

A: Many of the people of Israel married Hittites. Esau married a Hittite woman. The prophet Ezekiel told the people of Israel that God was not happy that they were marrying Hittites and Amorites.

Q: Did the Hittites believe in the God of Israel?

A: No. They believed in idols. This is why Ezekiel told them that God was not happy they married Hittites. God wanted the Israelites to marry people who believed in the God of Israel.

Q: What happened to the Hittites?

A: The Hittites became a weak nation. They were taken over by other people and they were conquered by the Assyrians. Soon after that the Assyrians took over Israel.

Q: Where did the Amorites live?

A: The Amorites lived in northwest Mesopotamia. The capital city for the Amorites was called Haran. Later they moved to Canaan and were the people that the Israelites had to fight to live in the promised land. The Bible says the Amorites were pagan people who did not worship the God of Israel. The Amorites worshiped many gods.

Q: Who were the most famous Amorite kings?

A: The most famous Amorite kings were Sihon and Og. The Israelites first destroyed the armies of Sihon and later beat the armies of Og. They had owned much land and were as famous as the Israelites.

Q: What happened to the Amorites?

A: The Amorites did not like the people of Israel. They joined with other kings and attacked the Israelite city of Jerusalem. Joshua fought a battle with the kings. He won a great victory, and the Amorites did not fight against Israel again.

Q: What does the name Hivite mean?

A: The name most likely means "village of nomads." The Hivites were people who lived in tents and who moved often. They lived in the land of Canaan. They were some of the people that God told the people of Israel to remove from the land of Canaan.

Q: What type of people were the Hivites?

A: They were a people who made their living trading. They did not seem to be warriors. During King Solomon's time, the Hivites became slaves of the Israelites.

Q: Who were the Ethiopians?

A: Ethiopians lived in a country south of Egypt, near the Nile River. Today we call this area Sudan. In the Bible it is often called the land of Cush.

Q: What does the Bible say about the land of Cush?

A: The Bible says that a river ran out from the Garden of Eden and divided into four branches. The second branch of the river is called Gihon, and it flows around the whole land of Cush.

Q: Who stole idols from her family?

A: Jacob was not getting along well with his brothers-in-law. He decided to move back to his home. He took his wives, Rachel and Leah, with him. Rachel stole some family idols from her father. She thought she deserved them as an inheritance.

Q: Who stole golden shields?

A: Shishak, the king of Egypt, attacked Jerusalem. He took all of the gold shields out of the house of the Lord. Later King Rehoboam replaced the gold shields with bronze shields.

Q: Who was accused of stealing a silver cup?

A: When Joseph became the vice-pharaoh in Egypt, his brothers came seeking food but they did not recognize Joseph. Joseph had one of his servants hide a silver cup in his brother Benjamin's sack. As his brothers started to leave Joseph accused them of stealing. He made the other brothers leave Benjamin. This was part of Joseph's plan to bring his family to Egypt.

Q: Who was the richest king?

A: The richest king was King Solomon. Other kings and queens would bring him silver, gold, garments, weapons, spices, horses, and mules. He was also the wisest man.

Q: Who was the first rich man mentioned in the Bible?

A: The first rich man to be mentioned in the Bible was Job. He owned 7,000 sheep, 3,000 camels, 500 yoke of oxen, 500 female donkeys, and many servants. He was a man who always served the Lord.

Q: Who showed off his wealth for six months?

A: King Ahasuerus (who is also known as Xerxes I) was very rich and powerful. His Persian kingdom stretched from India to Ethiopia. His royal throne was in the capital city called Susa. He decided to throw a banquet and display his wealth. The banquet lasted for six months.

Q: Who made the Philistines jealous because of his wealth?

A: Isaac, the son of Abraham, became a very wealthy man. His crops produced more than anyone else and he had many cattle. The Philistines became jealous of his riches. They tried to destroy his cattle by filling up his water wells. Isaac and his servants dug new wells and became even more wealthy.

Q: Where did the Babylonians live?

A: The Babylonians lived next to the Euphrates River in a land called Mesopotamia. Their capital was Babylon.

Q: What was Babylon famous for?

A: Babylon was famous for its hanging gardens. They were built by Nebuchadnezzar. The gardens had Persian plants and palm trees that were planted on terraces.

Q: What is King Nebuchadnezzar remembered for?

A: Nebuchadnezzar is famous for building much of Babylon. He is also remembered for putting Shadrach, Meshach, and Abednego into the fiery furnace. God struck Nebuchadnezzar with madness. He wandered in the fields like an animal for many years.

Q: Who was a famous Persian king?

A: King Darius. He put Daniel into the lion's den. Darius had been tricked by his governors and supervisors. God rescued Daniel by shutting the lions' mouths. Darius took Daniel out of the den and threw the men who had tricked him to the lions.

Q: Who was Jehoshaphat?

A: Jehoshaphat was a king who loved and trusted the Lord. One day the armies of Ammon, Moab, and Mount Seir declared war on Jehoshaphat. Jehosaphat was afraid and he prayed for God's help.

Q: Who was Hahaziel?

A: God sent a message to Jehoshaphat through a man named Hahaziel, who told Jehoshaphat to go out the next day to meet the enemy armies. God told Jehoshaphat that his army would not have to fight in the battle. God would rescue Jehoshaphat's army.

Q: What did Jehoshaphat do?

A: He had singers march in front of his army and sing praises to God. The next day Jehoshaphat, his singers, and his army marched out to meet the enemy kings. They had no idea how God would help them. They just trusted God for the victory.

Q: What did Jehoshaphat and his army find?

A: They found that all the enemy armies were dead. God had caused them to become greedy and fight each other. Jehoshaphat and his army did not have to fight at all. They picked up all the gold, silver, food, clothes, and weapons.

Q: Who was Ahab?

A: Ahab was a very bad king. He was greedy and selfish. He was married to wicked Queen Jezebel.

Q: Who was Naboth?

A: Naboth was a good man who owned property next to Ahab's summer home in Jezreel. Ahab would look over at Naboth's property. He wanted Naboth's property for his own. He tried to buy the property, but Naboth would not sell it.

Q: How did Jezebel get Naboth's land for Ahab?

A: Jezebel wrote a letter to the leaders of the city. She told them to make up false charges against Naboth and have him put on trial. Naboth lost the trial and was put to death. Then King Ahab took over Naboth's land.

Q: What did Elijah do when he heard about Naboth's death?

A: Elijah told King Ahab that God was very angry. He told Ahab that he would die a sudden and violent death. Ahab got scared. He put on sack cloth to punish himself and said he was sorry. God allowed him to live a little longer.

Q: Who were the Amalekites?

A: The Amalekites were an ancient group of people who lived about the time of Abraham. These people would wander the Negev Desert.

Q: When did Moses first meet the Amalekites?

A: Moses met the Amalekites at a place called Rephidim. It was there that the Amalekites attacked the people of Israel. They did not want them to have any water to drink. Joshua, the captain of the army, led the people of Israel to a great victory.

Q: What did God tell King Saul to do with the Amalekites?

A: God told King Saul to go to war with them. He said not to let anyone live, but Saul did not obey God. Saul kept all the best cattle and he let the king of the Amalekites live. The prophet Samuel told Saul it was better to obey God.

Q: What did the Amalekites do to the people they fought with?

A: The Amalekites would kill the people who were old and feeble. They would kill anyone who believed in God. They would destroy all the crops so that the people would starve.

Q: Who were the Ammonites?

A: The Ammonites were related to the Israelites through one of Lot's daughters. God told the people of Israel not to fight the Ammonites when they entered the land of Canaan.

Q: What were the Ammonites famous for?

A: The Ammonites were very fierce. They did not like the Israelites. They would murder people and they worshiped idols. In the city of Jabesh Gilead, the Ammonites put out the right eye of everyone who lived there. Both King Saul and King David defeated the Ammonites.

Q: What did the prophet Ezekiel say would happen to the Ammonites?

A: Ezekiel predicted that one day the Ammonites would be completely destroyed because of their wickedness.

Q: Who did the Ammonites worship?

A: Their main god was named Molech. But they may have also worshiped Baal, the Canaanite god. Baal was the god of storms and the king of all the other gods. Sometimes even the Israelites were tempted to worship Baal and the other gods.

Q: Who were the two giants who tried to kill David?

A: The first giant who tried to kill David was Goliath. He was over nine feet tall. David killed Goliath with a stone and sling. The second giant who tried to kill David was named Ishbi-benob. He was killed by Abishai, one of David's men.

Q: Who killed Goliath's brother?

A: Goliath had a brother named Lahmi. Elhanan, one of David's men, defeated Lahmi.

Q: Who was the giant with a huge bed?

A: The king of Bashan was a giant. His name was Og. He was the ruler of a large kingdom that had many cities. Og had an iron bed that was over 13 feet long and 6 feet wide.

Q: Who was the giant with six fingers and six toes?

A: When the Israelites went to war at Gath, they met a huge giant. He taunted and yelled at the soldiers of Israel. Jonathan, David's nephew, killed the giant. When the people came to see the dead giant they found that he had six fingers on each hand and six toes on each foot!

Q: Which prophet struck his enemies with blindness?

A: King Aram wanted to kill the king of Israel. He sent a great army to attack the city of Dothan. The prophet Elisha was in the city and saved the people by asking God to strike the army with blindness. Then Elisha led the blind army to Samaria and gave them back their sight. The army was so afraid of Elisha that they never attacked Israel again.

Q: In what city were all the men blinded?

A: The men of the city of Sodom were struck with blindness. It happened when two angels visited Lot. The men of the city wanted to hurt the two angels. The angels made the men blind. They then pulled Lot and his family out of Sodom. God sent fire on the city and destroyed it because of the wickedness of the people.

Q: Which king had his eyes put out by his enemies?

A: King Nebuchadnezzar attacked the city of Jerusalem. Zedekiah, the king of Jerusalem, and his army sneaked out of the city by night. They ran for their lives. Nebuchadnezzar's army caught Zedekiah. Nebuchadnezzar scattered Zedekiah's soldiers, killed his sons, and then put his eyes out and bound him in bronze chains. Zedekiah was then led back to Babylon.

Q: Who built most of the Tabernacle?

A: His name was Bezalel. He was the son of Uri, from the tribe of Judah. God gave him special abilities and understanding in all types of crafts. He knew how to work with gold, silver, and bronze. He also could carve stones and wood with very beautiful designs.

Q: Who is known for building cities with strong walls?

A: Jotham was only 25 years old when he became king. He became famous because he built cities in the mountains. He also built fortresses and towers in the forests. He was the king for 16 years.

Q: What builder had his workers wear weapons?

A: When Nehemiah rebuilt the walls of Jerusalem, his enemies were not happy. They said they were going to attack his workers. Nehemiah had the workers wear weapons while they worked in case the enemies attacked. He also put up a watch guard with a trumpet to warn the workers if anyone came near.

95

Q: What message did God give to Jeremiah?

A: God told Jeremiah to go to the house of a potter to learn a lesson. The potter would take a lump of clay and put it on a wheel, which he would turn. As the wheel went around, the potter used his hands to shape a pot.

Q: What happened when the potter found a rock in the clay?

A: When the potter found a rock, he stopped the wheel. Then he took the rock out and crushed the soft clay pot and started all over.

Q: What did God tell Jeremiah to do?

A: God told Jeremiah to buy a clay jar. He then told him to take the people and go out of the city of Jerusalem. The people followed Jeremiah. He took the jar and smashed it on the ground. The jar broke into many pieces.

Q: What lesson did God want Jeremiah to give the people?

A: Jeremiah told the people that their hearts were like the hard clay jar. He told them that they needed soft hearts that could be molded by God. God wanted to mold his people to do good deeds.

Q: What happened when good King Hezekiah died?

A: Manasseh became the king after the death of his father, Hezekiah. Manasseh was a very wicked king. He put idols in God's temple. He built altars to the god Baal.

Q: What happened to Manasseh?

A: The palace officials had him put to death. They made his son Josiah king. Josiah was only eight years old.

Q: How was Josiah different than Manasseh?

A: Josiah loved God and wanted to obey him. He wanted the people of Israel to serve God. Josiah decided to rebuild the temple. While the workers were repairing the building they found a special treasure. They found a lost copy of the law of God.

Q: What did Josiah do with the lost scroll?

A: Josiah read the law of God. He then tore down the altars to Baal. He called the priests back to Jerusalem. He brought back the celebration of the Passover. He got rid of all of the magicians and had the people follow the law of God. Josiah tried to follow God his whole life.

Q: Who was afraid of the people and did what they said?

A: When Moses went up to a mountain to talk to God, his brother, Aaron, stayed behind. When Moses did not return, the people told Aaron to make a golden idol. Aaron knew it was wrong, but he was afraid of the people and did what they said. God punished the Israelites because they disobeyed.

Q: Who was afraid of his father-in-law?

A: Jacob was afraid of his father-in-law, Laban. He thought that Laban would not let him keep his two wives, who were both the daughters of Laban. Jacob took his wives and fled. Laban followed them, but finally let them go.

Q: Who told his wife to pretend to be his sister?

A: Abraham traveled through Egypt with his family. He was afraid the Egyptians would kill him and take his wife because she was beautiful. He told his wife to tell the Egyptians that Abraham was her brother. The Egyptians took Abraham's wife. God punished the Egyptians with illness, so they gave her back to Abraham.

FAMILY WORSHIP & CUSTOMS

Q: How did families worship together in Bible times?

A: We do not know exactly. We do know that the fathers were responsible for their households, including the servants. Fathers would take the sacrifices to the priests.

Q: How did Israelite children learn about God?

A: Israelite children learned about God at home, from both their mothers and fathers. Parents taught their children wherever they were, sitting at home or walking along the road.

Q: Were Israelite children curious about God?

A: Yes. God told their parents to be ready to give them a good answer when the children asked about God. The Bible's truths were passed from mothers and fathers to daughters and sons to granddaughters and grandsons.

Q: "What does this mean?"

A: This was a question children would often ask their parents. They asked this when they read the Law and didn't understand it. Children in Jewish families today still ask their parents this question.

Q: What were Jewish prayers like?

A: They showed a great love and a great respect for God. The Bible records many beautiful prayers by people, including Hannah, David, Hezekiah, and Nehemiah. Many Jewish prayers today use the words of the Bible.

Q: What was the most important Jewish prayer?

A: This was a prayer called the Shema. *Shema* is the first Hebrew word of the prayer. It begins "Hear, O Israel, the Lord is our God, the Lord alone." It was important because it showed that the Jews believed in one God.

Q: When did people pray?

A: People prayed at any time of the day or night. There were prayers for morning and evening services in the Temple.

Q: What did people pray about?

A: They prayed about everything. Sometimes they sadly told God their troubles. Sometimes they joyfully thanked him for his goodness and help. Sometimes they asked him for help. Sometimes they asked God why there was suffering. These prayers even sound a bit angry.

Q: What was the Sabbath?

A: This was the day of rest at the end of the week. It reminded the Israelites that God had rested on the seventh day after creating the world in six days. No one was to work on the seventh day. When the Israelites were in the wilderness, God gave them a double amount of food on the day before the Sabbath. They saved half for the next day so they didn't have to work gathering and preparing it.

Q: How have Jews celebrated the Sabbath?

A: Many beautiful Sabbath customs have developed over the years—and Jews still do them today. Sabbath celebrations begin at sundown on Friday evening when families gather for a special meal. On Saturday morning, they go to synagogue. The rest of the day is spent resting, eating, and reading the Bible together. One Jewish group liked this day so much that they called it Princess Sabbath.

Q: Why did people celebrate the Sabbath?

A: The Sabbath was a very important day in Bible times. Not only could people rest and be refreshed, but it reminded them of God's creation—the world.

Q: What did the priests do?

A: The priests were the main religious leaders in Israel. They offered the sacrifices for people's sins. They could not forgive people's sins, but they were in the middle between the people and God. They were experts on God's Word, too.

Q: What did the high priest do?

A: The high priest was the highest religious authority in Israel. He had very special robes to wear. On his chest he had a breastplate with the names of the 12 tribes of Israel, showing he represented all people before God. He was the only person who could enter the holiest place in the Tabernacle and the Temple.

Q: Who were the Levites?

A: All the people whose ancestor was Levi, the son of Jacob, formed one of the 12 tribes of Israel. The Levites helped the priests do their work. They also took care of the Tabernacle.

Q: Were all priests faithful to God?

A: No. Most were faithful, but many did not worship God. A man named Micah hired a young Levite to be his personal priest. This was not the way they were to serve. The prophet Jeremiah angrily spoke of false priests.

Q: Who were the prophets?

A: Prophets were men and women that God sent to speak to the people. The prophets were usually not very popular. This was because the people had often disobeyed God and the prophets reminded them of that.

Q: What did the court prophets do?

A: Many kings liked to have their own prophets give them advice. These court prophets usually told the king only what he wanted to hear. They did not tell the kings what God wanted them to say.

Q: Who were the writing prophets?

A: They were the prophets whose words were written down and saved in books of the Bible. Some of the most famous were Isaiah, Jeremiah, Ezekiel, Hosea, and Amos. They brought stern messages to Israel, its kings, and even foreign nations. Sometimes they brought tender messages of hope.

Q: Who were the singing prophets?

A: Sometimes prophets lived together and prophesied by singing, playing music, and perhaps even dancing. Often they spoke with words nobody could understand.

Q: What did the judges do?

A: The judges were leaders who helped Israel defeat its enemies. They usually did this by leading an army. God raised up each judge when the Israelites cried out for help. There were judges for only a short period in Israel's history. Some of the judges also judged Israel in the way judges do today.

Q: Were the kings religious leaders?

A: The priests were the main religious leaders. But the kings also had religious duties. They were supposed to be examples for the people. They were to read and obey the Law, and to lead people in their faithfulness to God.

Q: Who were the scribes?

A: The scribes were official secretaries. In fact, they were some of the few people who could read and write. Their job was very important.

Q: Were there ever any false religious leaders?

A: Yes. There were false prophets and priests, and wicked kings and scribes. People also sometimes went to wizards, witches, or mediums for advice. These people did not make God happy.

Q: How did the Israelites celebrate their religious festivals?

A: The Israelites had many special days for worshiping God. Some were solemn days, when people confessed their sins. Others were happy celebrations of God's goodness. The three most important festivals were the feasts of Passover, Pentecost, and Tabernacles.

Q: What was the Passover Feast?

A: This was the spring festival of the barley harvest. It helped people remember when the Israelites escaped from Egypt. This was when God's angel of death killed all the oldest sons of the Egyptians. But the angel passed over the Israelite families who had put lamb's blood on their doorways. After that the Israelites left Egypt for the promised land. Families celebrated this together with a Passover meal. Jewish families still celebrate this today.

Q: What was the Feast of Pentecost?

A: This was a later spring festival celebrating the end of the grain harvest. It was also called the Feast of Weeks or the Feast of First-Fruits. It was a joyful festival. People stopped their work for the day. They brought offerings to God and made new promises to him that they would be faithful.

Q: What was the Feast of Tabernacles?

A: This was the great fall harvest festival. It lasted seven days. During this week the Israelites lived in tabernacles, which were little booths or huts. These were made out of branches and many of the grains that were harvested. This reminded the Israelites of the time they lived in tents in the desert. Even today many Jews still build tabernacles in their homes or their yards to celebrate this festival.

Q: What was the Feast of Unleavened Bread?

A: This was a week-long feast that came right after the Passover feast. It really was part of Passover. The Israelites did not do any work, and they made bread without any yeast (which makes dough rise). This reminded them of their escape from Egypt. They left Egypt in such a hurry that they could not even wait for their bread dough to rise.

Q: What was the Feast of Trumpets?

A: This was a day the Israelites rested and remembered what God had done for Israel. People also brought sacrifices to God. Many trumpets were blown on this day. It was held on the day of the new moon of the seventh month of the year (in the fall).

Q: What was the Day of Atonement?

A: This was a day of fasting (not eating) and rest every fall. It was the most important day for offering sacrifices for the nation's sins. The high priest carefully cleaned himself and his robes. Today it is called Yom Kippur.

Q: What was Hanukkah?

A: This festival celebrates a time after the Temple was captured by the Greeks. The Jews were able to take over the Temple again and re-dedicate it to God. The word *Hanukkah* means "dedication." The celebration is also called the Festival of Lights. This is because, according to Jewish tradition hundreds of years later, the Jews found a lamp in the Temple with only enough oil for one day. But the lamp stayed lit for eight days!

Q: What was the Festival of Purim?

A: Purim was a very joyful festival. It celebrated the Jews' great change of fortunes in the days of Esther. The Persian king had passed a law saying all Jews should be killed. Then he changed his mind, and said the Jews could kill anyone who attacked them. Jews have always enjoyed Purim, and even today they have fun parties to remember this time.

Q: Who built the Temple?

A: King David's son Solomon was the man who had the great Temple built in Jerusalem. David had helped him by gathering all of the building materials before he died. Then Solomon used thousands of workers to build it using tons of stone blocks and valuable woods. Precious stones, fabrics, and metals were also used.

Q: How was the Temple built?

A: The Temple Mount, where the Temple was built, was a holy place. Because of this, the workers did much of the work somewhere else. The huge stone blocks were cut and then they were taken to the Temple Mount and put in place. No hammers, axes, or iron tools were heard on the Temple Mount. This was to show respect for the holy place.

Q: Was the Temple an amazing building?

A: It certainly was! It was 3 stories high, 90 feet long, and 45 feet wide. It had two tall bronze pillars standing in front, with decorated fire-bowls on top. The stone walls were covered with fine wood and overlaid with gold.

Q: Why was the Temple important?

A: The Temple was God's house on earth. It had a room called the Most Holy Place (or Holy of Holies). This was where the Ark of the Covenant was kept. The Ark was a very important religious object.

Q: How did people worship at the Temple?

A: Hundreds of Levites were in charge of different parts of the worship services at the Temple. There were priests, with Levites helping them. There were musicians, gatekeepers, treasurers, and other officials.

Q: What was Temple music like?

A: It was usually joyful. Great choirs led people in singing psalms to God. The people played many musical instruments, including harps, lyres, flutes, trumpets, tambourines, and cymbals.

Q: What were the pilgrimage festivals like?

A: Three of the great annual festivals were called pilgrimage festivals. That meant that people had to go to Jerusalem to worship at the Temple. These festivals were the feasts of Passover, Pentecost, and Tabernacles.

114

Q: What was the Tabernacle?

A: The Tabernacle was a large tent. This was God's "home" when the Israelites were in the wilderness, before the Temple was built. In it was the Ark of the Covenant and other holy things. The Tabernacle was made of boards covered with layers of rich fabrics.

Q: What was the Tent of Meeting?

A: This was another name for the Tabernacle. This was where the people could meet God. But there was another tent called the Tent of Meeting, too. This was one that Moses would put outside the camp, and people could meet God there.

Q: Where else did people meet God?

A: People could talk with God anywhere. But there were also certain places where there were priests for people to go to. There was a place to worship God at Shiloh before Solomon built the Temple.

Q: Were there places in Israel where other gods were worshiped?

A: Yes. The most common places were called high places. These were places where Israelites worshiped false gods. They usually were on a hill.

Q: What were roads like in Bible lands?

A: Roads were usually just dirt paths. In rainy seasons they got very muddy. Sometimes armies made sturdier roads so that they could travel more easily. Later the Romans built very fine roads with smooth stones. Many of these roads still are in Israel today.

Q: How did people travel?

A: The people usually walked. Camels carried the heaviest burdens for merchants, traders, and other travelers. Donkeys were useful because they were very sure-footed, even in the mountains. Horses were mainly used in the army for pulling chariots. Mules were used by kings and the rich.

Q: Did people travel alone?

A: People usually traveled in caravans with camels and donkeys. People walking on foot could cover about 15 miles a day. Donkey caravans could travel about 20 miles a day. Fully loaded camel caravans could cover 18 to 20 miles a day. A man riding a fast camel could travel up to 70 miles a day.

Q: Where were the major trade routes in Palestine?

A: The most important road in Palestine was called the Way of the Sea. It connected Egypt with the great empires in Asia Minor and Mesopotamia. This road went north and south along the Mediterranean coast. Another important road was called the King's Highway. It ran north and south and was east of the Jordan River. Many local roads criss-crossed the countryside within Palestine.

Q: Were ships common in Bible times?

A: Yes. Ships and boats are mentioned many times in the Bible. The Israelites did not use these very much, but their neighbors did. Ships were used to carry goods to trade to faraway places. Ships were also used to carry armies. Israel's neighbors, the Phoenicians, were probably the most famous sailors in Old Testament times.

Q: What were ancient ships like?

A: Most ships in Old Testament times were small, maybe 50 feet long. They were sailing ships, but they also had crews for rowing. Warships usually had more rowers than trading ships.

Q: Did people live in caves in Old Testament times?

A: There are many caves in Palestine, and early in history people lived in them. But the Old Testament does not mention anyone living in caves except in emergencies.

Q: What kind of tents did people live in?

A: They lived in large tents that were probably like the tents that Arab shepherds live in today. These tents were made of goat's-hair fabric, which kept out the rain and the heat. There were three seven-foot-high tent poles in a row down the middle, and two rows on the outside. This made two rooms—one for women and children and one for men.

Q: What was life in tents like?

A: People who lived in tents were nomads, which means they did not stay in one place for longer than a few weeks or a few months. This was so they could always move to new pastures for their flocks.

Q: Who lived in tents?

A: Most early biblical people lived in tents. Abraham left his home in Ur and he set out with his family, servants, and flocks, and traveled to the land of Canaan.

120

Q: How many rooms did Israelite houses have?

A: During the time of Israel's kings, the most common type of house had four rooms. One room was long, which ran along the back wall. The other three rooms were side-by-side, next to the long room. People would enter the house through the middle room. This room was usually used as a courtyard.

Q: What did Israelite houses look like?

A: Most houses were small. They had flat roofs, and people would often sit on the roof to feel the cool afternoon breezes. Many houses had two stories. People climbed upstairs using stairways or ladders. The main living and sleeping quarters were on the second floor. Most windows in two-story houses were on the second story.

Q: What were Israelite houses made of?

A: Almost all were made of stones that were cut and stacked. Mud was then pushed between the stones. The walls were coated with water-proof plaster on the inside. The floors were made of hard-packed clay. Rich people's houses had floors paved with smooth stones. The roofs were made from wooden beams covered with branches.

121

Q: What were the Israelites' main foods?

A: The Israelites ate a lot of breads, grapes, and olive oil. They made many different foods using these three. They also ate many fruits and vegetables, as well as milk products (like cheese).

Q: What kind of breads did the Israelites eat?

A: The Israelites made their breads mostly from barley and wheat. They ground the grain into flour by using grinding stones. Then they mixed the dough. They would place it on heated stones, a griddle, or into a clay oven to bake.

Q: How did people use grapes?

A: Grapes were a cheap source of good food. People ate fresh grapes whenever they could. They also dried grapes and made raisins. They also made wine from grapes. Wine was served with meals and for special holidays. It was a luxury in Israel.

Q: How did people use olive oil?

A: Olive oil comes from olives of the olive tree. It was mixed with flour to make breads and cakes. Sometimes these were deep-fried in the oil. Olive oil also was used for burning in oil lamps. It was used to anoint people (like kings and priests).

Q: Did the Israelites eat much meat?

A: No. Meat was mainly a food for rich people. Sheep, cattle, and others were special foods. They were served to guests only on very special occasions. Meat was common in royal palaces, though, because kings could afford it.

Q: What did most people usually eat?

A: Besides the foods made from grain, grapes, and olive oil, people ate a lot of dairy products from cows and goats. They also ate many fruits. Figs, dates, and pomegranates were the most common.

Q: What was salt used for?

A: Salt was very common in Palestine. People got a lot of it from the Dead Sea. It was used to make food taste better. It was also used to keep food from spoiling in the hot climate.

Q: What did the Israelites eat when they were in the wilderness?

A: In the mornings, they ate a special food God had sent them called manna. Every day they woke up to find manna on the ground. It tasted like honey wafers. In the evenings, God sent quails into their camp. They could capture, roast, and eat them.

123

Q: What were the first clothes?

A: Before Adam and Eve sinned they did not wear any clothes, and they were not embarrassed. But after they sinned they were ashamed and made clothes for themselves. They made aprons out of fig leaves. Later God made them better clothes out of animal skins.

Q: How did men dress?

A: Most men wore loincloths around their waists and shirts or robes under their outer clothes. Their outer clothes included a colored garment. They also had outer cloaks or mantles. They used this for warmth, and slept in it at night. They took it off for work, and sometimes carried things in it. They wore cloth turbans or headpieces to protect them from the sun.

Q: How did women dress?

A: Women's clothing was similar to men's, but it was made of finer materials and had more colors. Women often used veils. They also had robes they wore under their outer garments. Their outer garments and headgear also protected them from the sun.

Q: What did the priests wear?

A: The priests' clothing was very colorful and expensive. Ordinary priests wore a cloth covering their hips and thighs and a long linen tunic with sleeves. They also wore a beautiful belt made of blue, purple, and scarlet cloth, and a kind of a turban. The high priest wore a very expensive breastplate made of gold and expensive linens. It had 12 precious stones in it, one for each tribe of Israel.

Q: What kind of shoes did people wear in Bible lands?

A: Sandals were the simplest and most common type of shoe. They were made of leather or woven reeds. They often were made of several layers of leather. Many shoes had uppers, too. These provided more protection against the cold in the winter and against stones, briers, and hot sand in the summer.

Q: What kind of shoes did soldiers wear?

A: Soldiers had to have much sturdier shoes than ordinary people. They marched long distances over very rough ground. They also needed more protection for their legs and feet. Roman soldiers wore high-topped leather shoes that were open at the toes, but reached up to the knee.

Q: What kind of jewelry did people wear?

A: People have worn jewelry since the beginning of history. Early in history jewelry was made of bone chips, shells, and colored stones. Later people used precious stones and metals. Many gold and silver necklaces, bracelets, earrings, and rings have been found in Bible lands, some with beautiful precious stones.

Q: What were popular jewels?

A: About 30 different types of precious stones are mentioned in the Bible. These include many-colored agates, reddish-purple amethysts, green emeralds, red garnets, clear diamonds, green jade, yellow-brown jasper, blue lapis lazuli, green malachite, white onyx, pale opals, shiny pearls, red rubies, blue sapphires, many-colored topaz, and blue-green turquoise.

Q: Did people wear hats?

A: Yes. But they were not hats we know. Both men and women wore cloth turbans or headpieces like long scarves to protect themselves from the sun. These were wrapped around their heads loosely. Women wore veils to hide their faces, too. Soldiers wore different kinds of helmets.

127

Q: What were the world's earliest schools like?

A: The oldest schools we know were in ancient Mesopotamia, around 2500 B.C. These were schools for scribes. Students copied texts over and over again on clay tablets. This helped them practice their writing. They studied many things besides writing, including geography, mathematics, and languages. Only rich people could send their children to scribes' school.

Q: Were there schools in ancient Israel?

A: The Old Testament does not mention schools. But many people could read and write. These included Moses, Samuel, David, Solomon, Isaiah, and Jeremiah's secretary, Baruch. Jewish scribes learned about the Law in the late Old Testament period. Ezra was the most famous scribe. Israelite children probably didn't go to school regularly.

Q: How did Israelite children learn?

A: Israelite children learned the trades and skills they needed from their parents. Fathers taught their sons about farming and other trades, such as carpentry. Mothers taught their daughters about taking care of a home. Both mothers and fathers taught their children about God and about living good lives. The home was the most important place to learn in Israel.

Q: When did synagogues come into being?

A: Synagogues were built after the Temple in Jerusalem was destroyed in 586 B.C. With the Temple gone, there was no place to offer sacrifices.

Q: How important was the synagogue?

A: The synagogue was the most important part of the community for Jews. Over time, every Jewish community had its own synagogue.

Q: What did people do during a synagogue service?

A: Ten adult men had to be present before a service could be held. The service had five parts. First a special prayer called the Shema was recited. Then there were general prayers, and after that the rabbi read from the Torah (the Law of Moses). Next was the reading from the prophets. They closed the service with the prayer of benediction.

Q: Where were the first schools started?

A: Sometime during the period between the Old and New Testaments Jewish schools for children were started in the synagogues.

129

Q: What deserts did the Israelites know?

A: Palestine is bordered by two great deserts. The great Arabian Desert stretches out to the east and southeast, and the Sinai Desert is to the south. In the southern part of Israel is the Negev wilderness, and the area east of Jerusalem is called the wilderness of Judea.

Q: What are the deserts like?

A: These deserts don't have sand dunes. Most of these deserts are flat. They are dry, but oases with springs and palm trees can be found. The wind blows sand across the flat, rocky surface.

Q: How did people live in the desert?

A: Desert dwellers raised sheep and goats. These animals provided them with food, such as dairy products and meat. They also provided them with materials for clothing and for their tents.

Q: Did people settle in the desert?

A: No. They had to take their flocks to different places to find water and to find new grazing grounds. Often they would live in the desert for six months and then go back to villages in the hill country.

Q: Where were the earliest cities?

A: The biblical city of Jericho was the world's first city—it is at least 7,000 years old. The first cities where writing was important were in Sumer (in what is Iraq today). The cities had walls around the temple areas. The streets were narrow, crooked, and not paved. Houses were crowded together.

Q: What were Israelite cities like?

A: These cities had walls for protection. Many city walls were very thick. The streets were crooked and narrow. Open areas were near the city gates. This was where people bought and sold things, and where judges judged cases.

Q: How did cities get water?

A: The cities were built near springs or streams that did not dry up in the summertime. If the spring was outside the city walls, people built water channels and tunnels to bring the water into the city.

Q: What was life in cities like?

A: Cities were very crowded. There were so many people that people had different jobs, instead of everyone having to be farmers or hunters.

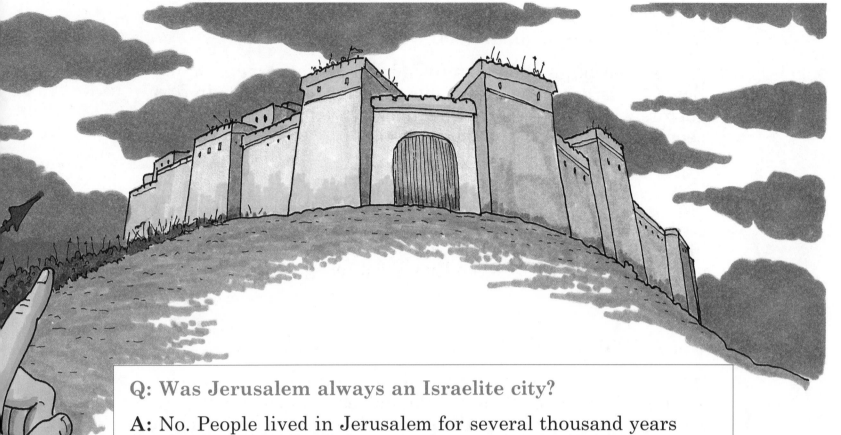

Q: Was Jerusalem always an Israelite city?

A: No. People lived in Jerusalem for several thousand years before David captured the city. The people who lived there when David took it were called Jebusites. The city was walled and very well protected. The Jebusites thought nobody could capture it.

Q: How did David capture Jerusalem?

A: The city was built on a hill, and its water supply was outside the walls. The Jebusites built a secret tunnel through the rock to the spring. David found out about the spring and the tunnel, and his men entered the city through these.

Q: What was Jerusalem like in biblical times?

A: In David's day it was small, about 15 acres. It was made larger by later kings. Solomon built the great Temple on a hill. The city was attacked many times, but was not captured until 586 B.C., when the Babylonians destroyed it.

Q: What were some of the different parts of the city?

A: The city expanded onto a hill west of where David's city was. The hill was where the rich people lived. Many different merchants sold their goods in Jerusalem.

Q: Were there medical doctors in Israel?

A: Yes. Joseph used doctors to embalm his father, Jacob, in Egypt. In Israel, King Asa of Judah sought medical help from doctors when he was sick. Usually God was the one who healed people in Old Testament times, though.

Q: Were there nurses in Israel?

A: The midwife was very important in Israel. Midwives were like visiting nurses or public health workers. The Hebrews had professional midwives when they lived in Egypt at the time Moses was born.

Q: How did the Israelites keep from getting sick?

A: Many parts of the Law that God gave the Israelites were good medical advice. Many of the unclean animals they were not to eat carry different kinds of germs. There were many laws about carefully washing your body.

Q: What medicines were used in Israel?

A: There were not many good medicines for serious diseases in biblical times. Sometimes people drank wine to help their stomachs. Most medicines were ointments that were rubbed on sores. These ointments protected the people from the sun and bugs.

Q: What were some jobs people had in Israel?

A: The most important jobs provided food and shelter. Farmers and shepherds provided food for people to eat. Women prepared and cooked the food and made cloth out of animal skin for tents. Builders built houses and palaces for people to live in.

Q: Were there any business people in Israel?

A: Yes. Many merchants made products to sell. These would often be sold by the city gate. In larger cities, craftsmen of the same trade lived in the same area—there would be the potters' section of town, the food market, and the bakers' street.

Q: What were some of the trades?

A: Carpenters and woodworkers made homes, tools for farming, and weapons for war. Many workers worked in quarries and mines. They took stone, salt, iron, copper, gold, and other minerals out of the earth. Many workers became metal-workers—shaping tools, weapons, and jewelry.

Q: What other jobs were important?

A: Religious jobs were very important—many priests and Levites worked in the Temple. A king's household needed thousands of workers to support the royal lifestyles.

Q: When did people begin farming?

A: The Bible says that the first man, Adam, was a farmer. After Adam and Eve sinned, farming became more difficult. Cain, their son, was also a farmer.

Q: What were the most important crops in Israel?

A: The most important crops were grain, oil, and wine. The most important grains were barley and wheat. Oil came from olive trees. Wine and raisins came from grapes.

Q: What were Israelite farms like?

A: The kings and rich people owned large estates and they needed workers to do the farming. These large farms had many pastures for their cattle and flocks, and many fields for their crops. Most Israelite farmers owned small plots of land.

Q: Where did Israelite farmers live?

A: They did not live on farms like we know today. They lived in small, crowded villages not far from their fields. Usually these villages were within a few miles of a walled city. That way people in the villages could be protected by the city.

Q: How did farmers plant their crops?

A: First the farmers scattered seeds in the field. Then they plowed their fields with a hand plow. Plows were made of wood and they had a cone-shaped metal tip that went into the ground. Plows were usually pulled by a team of oxen.

Q: What did farmers do after planting?

A: They had to protect the crops from birds and animals. They also had to dig out weeds. They used hoes made of two sticks.

Q: How did farmers harvest their crops?

A: The harvest had to be brought in quickly, so everybody helped. Some workers cut the stalks of grain with curved wooden sickles with iron blades. Other workers collected the grain and tied them into bundles, called sheaves.

Q: Were the farmers done farming after harvesting?

A: No. They had to *thresh* and *winnow* the crops. They threshed by beating the grain with sticks or grinding it under big stones. This separated the kernels of grain from the straw. They winnowed by throwing everything into the air so the wind could blow away the straw (or chaff). The heavier grain fell to the ground and was saved.

Q: How were grapes farmed?

A: Grapes grew on vines in vineyards. The farmers had to hoe the ground and trim the vines, taking off dead branches. They trimmed (or pruned) with small knives with hooked blades. The grapes were then picked at harvest time.

Q: What were grapes used for?

A: They were used for making wine. They were dumped into small basins cut out of stone. The juice was squeezed out by people stepping on the grapes. Then the juice was placed in deep vats to ferment into wine. Grapes also were dried in the sun to make raisins. Sometimes lots of raisins were pressed into raisin cakes.

Q: How were olives farmed?

A: Olives grew on trees in orchards. These short, twisted trees did not need much attention until harvest time. Olives were usually picked by hand, but sometimes they couldn't be reached. When this happened, the farmers had to shake them off or beat the branches with long twigs or sticks. The olives then were crushed and pressed so that the oil could be collected.

Q: What was everyday life like in Israel?

A: For most people, life was hard. Fathers and children worked hard in the fields raising crops or animals, and whole families helped out during harvest or other important times. Houses were small, and many people slept in one room. People usually slept on straw mats on the floor. Mothers worked hard preparing and cooking food and taking care of their families.

Q: What was life like for children in Israel?

A: Children were important in Israel. They were a blessing from God. Parents loved their children and taught them about God. Children also worked hard. They helped their parents.

Q: Did Israelite children ever play games?

A: Yes. Many children's toys have been found in Israelite towns. These include whistles, rattles, marbles, dolls, and toy animals. Israelite children also kept pets, such as birds.

Q: Did adults ever play games?

A: Yes. Even though life was hard for most people, they still found time for games. Adults ran, wrestled, shot slingshots or bows and arrows. Many of these games helped them practice their military skills, in case of a war.

HOW THE BIBLE CAME TO BE

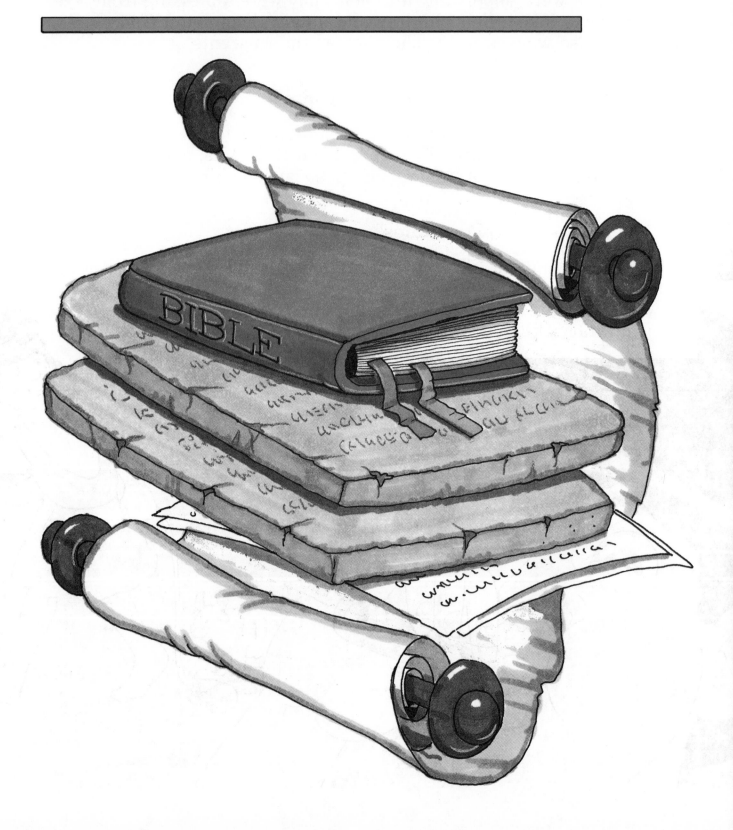

Q: Who wrote the Bible?

A: God gave the words and ideas to many different people. Ezekiel was a priest, and David and Solomon were kings. Others were ordinary people. Amos was a shepherd and Matthew was a tax collector.

Q: How did God give his words to the Bible's authors?

A: Sometimes the writers had dreams in which God told them what to write. Sometimes God spoke out loud to them, or he put an idea in their minds and they wrote it in their own words. Sometimes God told them to copy parts of their books from other books and then to make their own comments on those parts.

Q: How did the Bible's authors write?

A: Many probably did their own writing, but others told their words to a scribe or secretary who wrote them down. Some authors' words may have been collected and written by their followers.

Q: When was the Bible written?

A: The earliest parts of the Bible (Genesis to Deuteronomy) were written over 3,000 years ago. The last parts of the Old Testament (such as the books of Chronicles) were written about 1,000 years later.

Q: What is the Old Testament?

A: It tells the stories of God working with the children of Israel. It tells about the Messiah who was to come later to save the world. The word testament means "covenant," so the Old Testament means the "old (or first) covenant" that God made with his people.

Q: How many books are in the Old Testament?

A: There are 39 books in the Old Testament. Roman Catholic and many Eastern Orthodox churches include another 12 to 16 books in the Old Testament. These are usually called the books of the Apocrypha.

Q: Are Jewish and Christian Bibles the same?

A: No. The Jewish Bible contains the same 39 books as the Protestant Old Testament, but in a different order. Jews call it the Bible or the *Tanakh*.

Q: Are there other Jewish writings from biblical times?

A: Yes. The Jews wrote many books. There are books about the Bible, devotional books, other stories of biblical heroes, and more.

Q: Was the Bible first written as a book?

A: No. Each book of the Bible was written on a scroll. Most scrolls were about 10 to 12 inches wide and up to 35 feet long! They were rolled up around two wooden rollers.

Q: When were books invented?

A: The first real books were invented shortly after Christ lived. Scrolls were cut into page-size sheets and sewn together. The first books were sewn down the middle, but this made them hard to write on. Later they were sewn along one edge.

Q: What was the Bible written on?

A: Most of the Bible was written on papyrus or parchment. Papyrus is made of dried reeds. Many reeds were laid next to each other and crushed together, and then dried out. We get our word "paper" from papyrus. Parchment is made of animal skins, which were stretched, scrubbed, dried, and sometimes bleached.

Q: Was all writing done on papyrus or parchment?

A: No. Many important documents were carved into stone. Many other texts were written on clay tablets. Many letters were written in ink on broken pieces of pottery.

Q: How was the Bible passed down over many centuries?

A: For hundreds of years the Bible was copied by hand. Skilled and specially trained scribes copied it. If a scribe made too many mistakes the entire scroll or book was destroyed. Later scribes were so careful that they knew exactly how many words were in each book of the Old Testament!

Q: Who were the scribes?

A: Scribes copied and taught the Scriptures. They were very respected in Israel. They could read and write, and they became teachers of the Law for the Jews.

Q: Did people in Bible times have Bibles like we do?

A: No. Most people couldn't read and write. They learned what the Bible said when the priests or the scribes read it to them. Public readings of the Scriptures were very important in ancient Israel.

Q: What are the earliest copies of the Bible that we have?

A: Hundreds of scrolls and pieces of scrolls were found near the Dead Sea between 1947 and 1956. These include many copies of books from the Old Testament. They are the earliest copies of parts of the Bible.

Q: What happened when a copy of the Bible wore out?

A: The Jews would not throw it away. They collected worn-out and damaged copies of their Bible. Then they stored them in special storerooms in their synagogues called *genizahs*, which is Hebrew for "hiding places." Then they buried them in special ceremonies.

Q: How was the Bible copied during the Middle Ages?

A: Jewish scribes and Christian monks kept copying the Bible by hand during the Middle Ages, which is sometimes called the Dark Ages. This is not a very accurate term because much learning was taking place then. Jewish scribes produced beautiful copies of the Old Testament. They had elaborate calligraphy (special artistic writing) and they used different-colored inks. They even drew beautiful pictures in the margins and at the beginning of chapters.

Q: Why were printing presses invented?

A: Copying books by hand was very tiring. It took a long time, and people made mistakes. When the printing press was invented, hundreds and even thousands of copies could be printed, each exactly the same. This made it possible for almost anyone to have a Bible.

Q: Who printed the first Bible?

A: A German named Johann Gutenberg printed the first Bible. It was written in Latin. He worked for many years inventing his printing press. People called the results of his work *artificial writing*. Gutenberg's Bible was printed in 1456.

Q: How was the first Bible printed?

A: Gutenberg's printing press had printing plates, which were held in a "bed." Then the printer rolled ink over them and blank sheets of paper were pressed onto them.

Q: How is the Bible produced today?

A: Modern Bibles are printed using space-age technology. The pages are still pressed onto blank sheets of paper, but now it is lightning-fast!

Q: What language was the Old Testament written in?

A: It was written in two languages. Most of the Old Testament was written in Hebrew. Parts of the books of Ezra and Daniel were written in Aramaic.

Q: How is Hebrew written?

A: Hebrew is written from right to left. It used to be written without any vowels, spaces between words, or punctuation. Here is "Mary had a little lamb" written this way: bmllttldhrm.

Q: What was the Hebrew alphabet like?

A: The earliest Hebrew alphabet used pictures to stand for letters. The first letter of the alphabet was a picture of an ox's head. Over hundreds of years the letter changed until it looked like an *A*. We got our A from Hebrew!

Q: How did people find passages in the Old Testament?

A: It was difficult. The Old Testament was first written without any chapter or verse numbers. The first verse numbers were put in by Jewish scribes.

Q: Is Hebrew like English?

A: A bit. *Aleph, Beth, Gimel,* and *Daleth* are the first letters of the Hebrew alphabet. These are like our letters A, B, G, and D.

Q: Did Adam speak Hebrew?

A: No, probably not. All languages change over the years, so Adam probably spoke a language that we don't know any more.

Q: Did people have different accents in biblical times?

A: Yes. People living east of the Jordan River sounded slightly different from those who lived west of it. During one war, the easterners used the word *shib-bo-let* (which means "ear of grain") as a password. The enemy didn't pronounce it the same way. They said *sib-bo-let,* so they gave themselves away and were captured.

Q: Have Jews always spoken Hebrew?

A: No. At the end of the Old Testament period most Jews began speaking Aramaic. The rabbis were the only ones who could read Hebrew, so it became a "dead" language. About 100 years ago Hebrew was made into a spoken language again. Today it is the language of Israel.

151

Q: Did all Jews speak Hebrew?

A: No. Shortly after Old Testament times Jews no longer spoke Hebrew. Most spoke Aramaic or Greek, so their Scriptures were translated into these languages.

Q: What was the Bible that Jesus used?

A: When Jesus lived the New Testament had not been written. The Bible he and his disciples read was the Old Testament. It had been translated into Greek, since people who spoke many different languages could all read Greek.

Q: Why was Latin such a popular language?

A: Latin was the language of the Roman Empire. In A.D. 313, Constantine the Great made Christianity the religion of the Empire. After this Christians used Latin in their churches.

Q: Is the Bible available in every language now?

A: No. There are more than 6,000 known languages in the world today, and the Bible has been translated into about 2,000. Most of the other languages are of small, remote tribes or groups. Many organizations are working today to translate the Bible into the languages that are left.

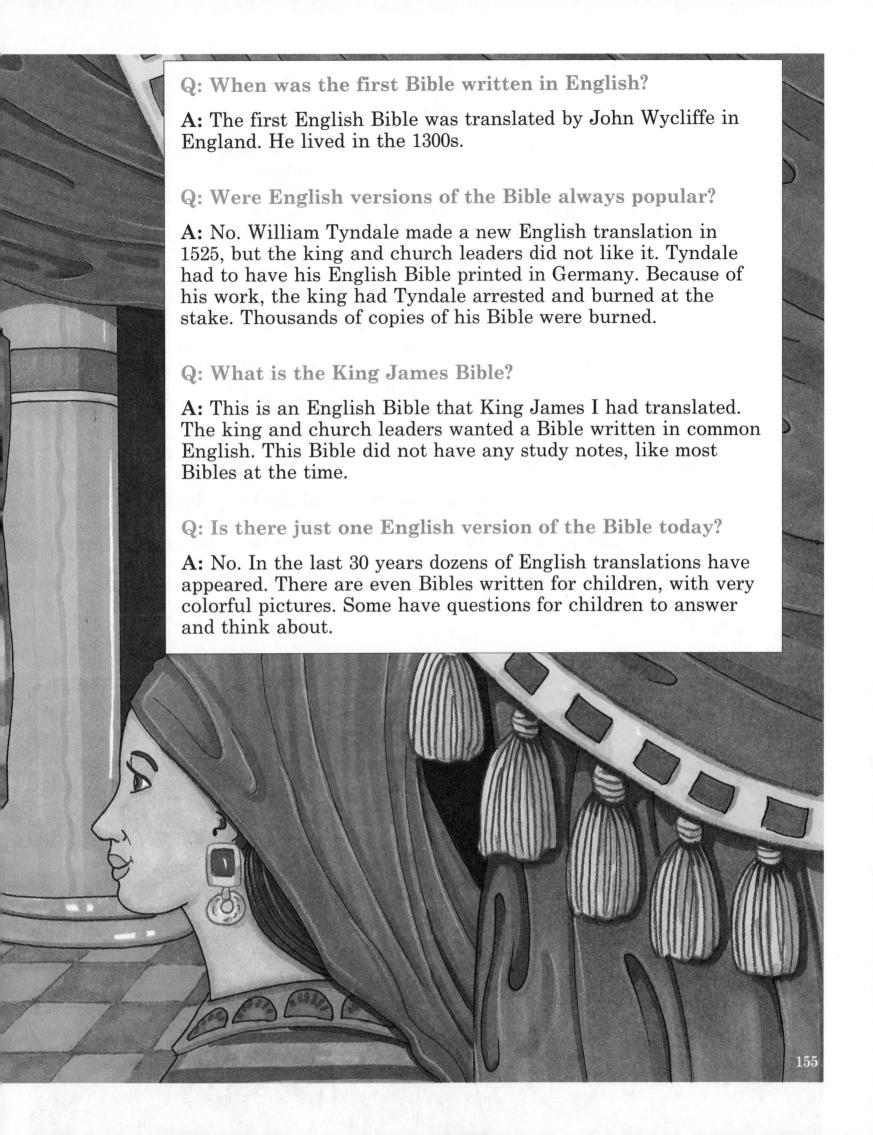

Q: When was the first Bible written in English?

A: The first English Bible was translated by John Wycliffe in England. He lived in the 1300s.

Q: Were English versions of the Bible always popular?

A: No. William Tyndale made a new English translation in 1525, but the king and church leaders did not like it. Tyndale had to have his English Bible printed in Germany. Because of his work, the king had Tyndale arrested and burned at the stake. Thousands of copies of his Bible were burned.

Q: What is the King James Bible?

A: This is an English Bible that King James I had translated. The king and church leaders wanted a Bible written in common English. This Bible did not have any study notes, like most Bibles at the time.

Q: Is there just one English version of the Bible today?

A: No. In the last 30 years dozens of English translations have appeared. There are even Bibles written for children, with very colorful pictures. Some have questions for children to answer and think about.

Q: What types of books are in the Old Testament?

A: The Old Testament has many different kinds of books. These include books of law, history, songs, wise teachings, and prophecy. We can find instructions, stories, parables, lists, letters, family histories, songs and victory hymns, legal documents, and even riddles in these books.

Q: What are the books of law?

A: These are the books of Exodus, Leviticus, Numbers, and Deuteronomy. They have all the laws that the Israelites were to follow. These include instructions for all people, such as the Ten Commandments. They also include laws just for the Israelites, such as what foods they could and couldn't eat.

Q: What are the historical books?

A: These are the books that have the stories of the Israelites. They include the books of Genesis, Exodus, Numbers, and Joshua through Esther. They tell the story of how God chose Abraham and his children down through the ages. God wanted to bless them, and to bless the world through them. Abraham's descendants did not always obey God, but God was always faithful to them.

Q: What are the poetic books?

A: Many of the Bible's books have poetry. The Book of Psalms is the longest of these. The word *psalm* means "a song sung with a stringed instrument." The psalms were sung by the Jews in Bible times. Most psalms are praises to God. Some psalms tell God about people's troubles.

Q: What are the wisdom books?

A: These are books of wise teachings. The Book of Proverbs has wise, common-sense advice for how to live. Ecclesiastes asks deep questions, such as "What is life all about?" The Book of Job talks about why innocent people sometimes suffer.

Q: What are the books of prophecy?

A: The prophets were God's preachers. Their books told people they should stop sinning and turn to God or be punished. The prophets usually were not popular, since people didn't like to hear bad news. The prophets also told people that God loved them and would save them if they turned to him. They also spoke of the wonderful kingdom God was going to set up at the end of time.

Q: How were the Bible's stories passed along?

A: Many Bible stories probably were memorized before they were written down. But they all were written down at some time. This was usually done soon after the events in the stories. Then they were read and told to each new generation. Imagine storytellers delighting audiences in public squares and around campfires with the great stories of history!

Q: Did parents teach their children about the Bible?

A: Yes. One of the most important things parents were supposed to do was to tell their children about God. They did this by telling the stories of how God had blessed and saved his people time after time. They also told their children about how God wanted them to live.

Q: Were any Bible books written for children?

A: Yes. Children can read and understand many of the Bible's stories about God's people. Also, the Book of Proverbs has many good pieces of advice written especially for children. They were given by a father and mother to their children.

Q: What parts of the Bible were sung?

A: The psalms are the most well-known part of the Bible that were sung. These were sung as part of Israel's worship of God at the Temple. King David wrote some of the psalms himself.

Q: Did people just sing in the Temple?

A: No. People sang songs at other times and in other places also. Moses and his sister, Miriam, led the people in a thanksgiving song when the Israelites escaped the Egyptians when the Red Sea parted. Deborah, a prophet, and the general Barak sang a great victory song over their Canaanite enemies.

Q: How good were the Bible's storytellers?

A: They were very good. The story of Ruth is a beautiful love story. The stories of Joseph and of Esther and Mordechai are very inspiring. The story of Ehud killing Jabin is so intense it is almost disgusting. Many of the stories about David have drama, suspense, humor, and great details.